PUSHED OUT

PUSHED OUT

CONTESTED DEVELOPMENT
AND RURAL GENTRIFICATION
IN THE US WEST

RYANNE PILGERAM

UNIVERSITY OF WASHINGTON PRESS | *Seattle*

Pushed Out was made possible in part by a grant from the Capell Family Endowed Book Fund, which supports the publication of books that deepen our understanding of social justice through historical, cultural, and environmental studies.

Design by Katrina Noble
Composed in Iowan Old Style, typeface designed by John Downer
Map by Chelsea M. Feeney, www.cmcfeeney.com

25 24 23 22 21   5 4 3 2 1

Printed and bound in the United States of America

UNIVERSITY OF WASHINGTON PRESS
uwapress.uw.edu

LIBRARY OF CONGRESS CATALOGING-IN-PUBLICATION DATA

Names: Pilgeram, Ryanne, author.
Title: Pushed out : contested development and rural gentrification in the US West / Ryanne Pilgeram.
Description: Seattle : University of Washington Press, [2021] | Includes bibliographical references and index. |
Identifiers: LCCN 2020047577 (print) | LCCN 2020047578 (ebook) | ISBN 9780295748689 (hardcover) | ISBN 9780295748696 (paperback) | ISBN 9780295748702 (ebook)
Subjects: LCSH: Gentrification—Idaho—Dover. | Dover (Idaho)—Economic conditions. | Dover (Idaho)—Social conditions.
Classification: LCC HT177.D68 P55 2021 (print) | LCC HT177.D68 (ebook) | DDC 307.1/4120979696—dc23
LC record available at https://lccn.loc.gov/2020047577
LC ebook record available at https://lccn.loc.gov/2020047578

To my mom

CONTENTS

PREFACE

Outside of North Idaho (where it's never called Northern Idaho), most people have probably never heard of Dover. Sixty miles from the Canadian border and fifty miles from the nearest interstate, Dover is not a place you stumble upon. People who make the trek off the interstate and head north head to the picturesque beach town of Sandpoint, Idaho, three miles east of Dover, or Schweitzer Mountain, fifteen miles to the north, to ski. For decades, you might only have noticed Dover because the narrow highway severed the town into two parts: a sliver of town with the post office on one side, and most of the houses, the mill, the community center, and the church on the other. But even that's changed now. Today, a desperately needed new bridge and a widened highway mean you can speed over the community. If you keep your eyes on the road, you might never even realize you're passing over a town.

My interest in Dover started decades ago, when my mom, my sister, and I moved to a log house on a slough in a sort of no-man's-land between Sandpoint and Dover. I was starting my first year of high school, the daughter of a suddenly single mother. As a fifth-generation Montanan, I hated pretty much everything about Idaho. There's a popular sentiment in Sandpoint that the first time you come across the Long Bridge—the two-mile bridge that crosses the lake and offers dazzling views of the mountains—you never want to leave. But we had come in the back way, and it would be months before I crossed the Long Bridge, so I didn't find it difficult to hate Sandpoint. That said, it was hard to dislike Dover, though I tried.

I lived only a mile from Sandpoint High School, but I mostly took the bus to and from the school during my first year. After school, the bus made a wide, nine-mile loop, up Pine Street Hill and along gravel mountain roads, dropping off handfuls of students who lived in houses tucked into the woods. Thirty minutes later, we would finally pop out on Highway 2. We would make a quick trip up the highway, following the river west, then the bus would flip around in a gravel pit and finally head back east to make its two stops in Dover. Most of the students riding that route lived in Dover, but the Sandpoint High School bus routes put them at the bottom of the priority list. My sister and I were the last kids off the bus as it headed from Dover back toward Sandpoint, but the bumpy ride (always either too hot or too cold) was always better than walking.

Some of the people I met on "the Dover bus" have remained close friends. Dover, Idaho, is where I took those fragile first steps from adolescence into adulthood. For example, Dover is where I had my first (and only) car accident, a fender bender that happened at about five miles an hour. As is the custom in North Idaho, we left our bus riding behind when we got our daytime driver's licenses at age fourteen and a half. We all got crappy jobs and beater cars, and then proceeded to plow into each other's mailboxes when we attempted to back out of long, icy driveways with very little experience (our parents looking on in horror from front windows).

Dover is also where I fell in love for the first time, with a boy whose recently divorced mom had moved out to a trailer that she covered in art she created from the driftwood and rocks outside her front door. It is where my mom, my sister, and I would picnic in the summer on a rare day that one of us was not working: a bucket of fried chicken on the sandy beach in the shade of the cottonwoods. And it is where I stood with a group of young women as we tried to support our friend who was mourning the death of her parents, taken much too young. We placed flowers in the cold water of the river that morning.

I left for college in 1999. Perhaps it was youthful inexperience, but the slow life of North Idaho, where mills closed, maybe even burned down, but the piles of sawdust didn't go away, made it difficult for me to imagine

Dover as anything much more than a former mill town. I assumed it would become a bedroom community for Sandpoint, a place offering inexpensive house and a short drive to work.

I had just started working on my doctorate in sociology when I learned about the old mill development. Being two states away in the days before social media, the news came as a shock. Perhaps it should not have. The region frequently found its way onto "best places to live" lists, and the site was, in most ways, perfectly situated for development.

I earned my PhD in sociology in 2010 and was fortunate to land a position as an assistant professor at the University of Idaho. The research component of my job led me to study the lives of farmers in Idaho, but my interest in Dover remained. When I would go back to visit my mom, we would have dinner at the new restaurant that had been built there or just drive around to take in the changes. It was only after I earned tenure that I felt ready to turn my interest in the community into a professional undertaking. Because of my work on farming and agriculture, I had been asked to introduce a panel as part of a conference on the rural West. Listening to the scholars on that panel, particularly the brilliant Dr. Jennifer Sherman, I began to put the changes in Dover into a sociological and historical framework that I had not before. As I listened, the changes in Dover seemed nearly a perfect example of the phenomenon the researchers were discussing at that panel: rural gentrification.

It was these threads coming together that led me to write this book. I wanted to bring my experience as a researcher to a community that I very much cared about and delve deeply into the changes that had taken place. It is one thing to have the USDA classify your community in a particular way, but it doesn't tell you very much about the ins and outs of those changes. I was interested in the experiences of folks who'd been in Dover for ninety years or more, as well as those who were new. I was also interested in understanding how the city had decided to rezone the land, since Dover seemed unique because of the relative power the city had over the land. Especially in places like Idaho, private property owners often have few restrictions on how they use their land. In Dover, however, the development was located within the city, and so the city council had the power to veto it. So why would some in the community seem to embrace the development?

As I worked to understand this process, I became particularly grateful to the many people who opened their homes and offices to me and who shared a cup of coffee with me (especially with hot chocolate added). I am grateful to the recordkeepers and storykeepers who helped me track down the next piece of information that I needed in this puzzle. I have put my energies into being fair to the many voices that make up this book while being clear about the process of development in Dover.

This book is for all the people who made this project possible, but especially young people, who will be the next generation to create communities. I hope that this book helps them imagine ways we can create spaces where everyone can thrive.

ACKNOWLEDGMENTS

In many ways the seed of this book was planted by my much-beloved mentor, Dr. Byron Steiger. It was in his classroom at Pacific University that I was introduced to the sociological imagination and began to see the world in all its complexity. It was under his care that I also began to imagine myself as someone who might have something to say that would be worthy of being read. For that and so many other reasons, I am so deeply grateful.

To Drs. Ellen Scott and Jocelyn Hollander at the University of Oregon, who are also treasured mentors and friends, thank you for all the lessons you patiently walked me through, but most especially all the time you put into teaching me the art and craft of taking data and shaping it into a narrative.

Thank you also to the University of Idaho's College of Letters, Arts and Social Sciences' Kurt O. Olsson Early Career Research Fellowship and to the John Calhoun Smith Memorial Fund, which helped to make this book possible.

To my wonderful colleagues at the University of Idaho, and especially the sociology faculty, Drs. Kristin Haltinner, Leontina Hormel, Dilshani Sarathchandra, and Debb Thorne, thank you for giving me the space to finish this book, for encouraging me to take a sabbatical even when it meant scheduling was more complicated, and for your constant cheer-leading. I am so lucky to work with you all. And thank you to my friends and colleagues who helped me celebrate each small achievement as I worked on this project, especially Jenn Ladino.

To Andrew Berzanskis, thank you for being such a dedicated editor, in particular for your general sense of humor and for being so understanding about what it was like to try and finish a book during a pandemic with children milling about. You are also the promptest emailer I've ever worked with, and that, combined with your support and clear advice, made it so much easier to finish this project.

To the people of Dover, I don't even know where to start. I am so profoundly grateful to you. Thank you for sharing your stories, your time, your homes, and your beloved community with me.

Thank you to the recordkeepers. Your archives kept this project moving forward. Special thanks to Teena Weisz, whose careful record of Dover's history made many early parts of this book possible.

To my loud, wonderful, and weird siblings, nieces, nephews, and fake-siblings: Zane, Jaidyn, Zane, Miley, and Riley; Casey, John, Samih, and Runa; Doug; and Yvette. I don't know what you did to help me, but just the same, without you I would have so few stories to tell—and we all know that if you end up with a good story, it is pretty much always worth the discomfort. I know one of you will find a single typo in this book and never let me live it down. Just the same, I would be lost without the lightness you bring to my life. Thanks for letting me boss you all around, forever.

To my children: Alden, your curiosity about the world, your questions, your insights, and your general sense that knowledge is for all of us reminded me that I could learn outside my comfort zone as this project kept growing. Will, your humor and gentleness toward people, animals, and bugs pushed me to write a book that focused on the goodness of people. Fern, your tenacity and fearless made me braver than I sometimes felt. Together, you have sanded away my roughest parts and, I am sure, have left me far better than you found me. Thank you for the fullness you bring to our life.

To Russ, who is empirically speaking, the world's best husband, you have stepped up in a million ways to make possible this book, my career, and ultimately the life we have created together. I do not know who I would be without your kindness, constant support, and love. I am so grateful for the grace you show the people around you and the grace you show me as we navigate the many demands on our time and attention (most especially the three names previously mentioned). I'm not sure it is right to want to "have it all," but certainly everything I do have is because you are at my side.

To my mom, Marcia, your support as I wrote this book is nothing short of a miracle. You not only helped me find people to interview but also provided me a warm bed, extremely tasty food and drink, and free babysitting as I conducted the fieldwork and wrote. I would be lost without your love, your humor, and your encouragement in this project (and all the others you have supported me through). You have always shone your light upon me so brightly that I came to believe I was worthy of it. Please always do that.

PUSHED OUT

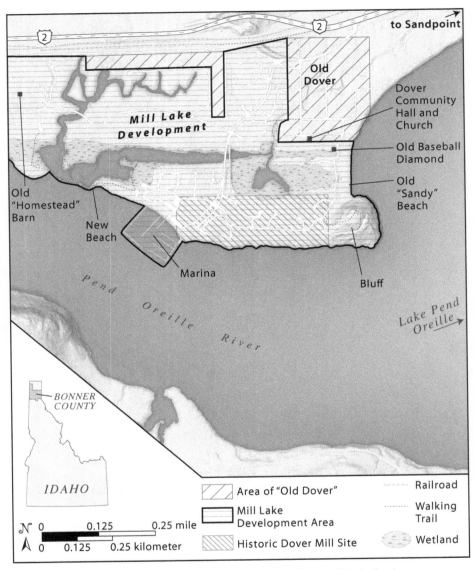

to Sandpoint

Old
Dover

Dover
Community
Hall and
Church

Old Baseball
Diamond

Old
"Sandy"
Beach

*Mill Lake
Development*

Old
"Homestead"
Barn

New
Beach

Marina

Bluff

P e n d   O r e i l l e   R i v e r

*Lake Pend
Oreille*

*BONNER
COUNTY*

IDAHO

N
A

0   0.125   0.25 mile
0   0.125   0.25 kilometer

⬚ Area of "Old Dover"
▭ Mill Lake
Development Area
▨ Historic Dover Mill Site

Railroad

Walking
Trail

Wetland

Map of Dover, Idaho, showing some of the key places discussed in the book.

Introduction

Welcome to Dover

EVERY MONTH, "THE Dover Girls" meet to share a potluck lunch and work on a project at the community hall. One of this week's projects was making blankets for what one of them termed "abused women." The Dover Girls—a group of older women who all grew up there—had spent a lifetime together as friends and neighbors, raising children and burying husbands, so sharing the afternoon with them felt like being let in on a secret. The women teased and joked, filling and refilling their plates with casseroles, salads, rolls, and desserts and encouraging me to do the same. They were completely at ease with each other. After lunch, they got to work on their tasks: sewing dresses to send to Africa and making blankets for a domestic violence shelter. There was a matter-of-factness to the discussion. They were making blankets for these women because, as Sharon Miller, who was in her eighties and had lived in Dover since she was child, explained, "when men are laid off and at Christmastime," they tend to drink too much and "knock women around."

The community hall hosting this event, along with most of the other homes and buildings in town, was originally built for a different mill town in the area, but when that mill burned down in 1922, the mill's owner, A. C. White, sent a flotilla of buildings upriver to the site of a new mill and what would eventually become Dover, Idaho. If the burnt-orange percolating coffee pot was any indication, the community hall, like much of old Dover, had not seen many changes since the buildings were moved.

The walls were the soft industrial green that had gone out of style but is now back in fashion. In places, large swaths of the green paint was bubbling and peeling away, a sign of water damage and age.

But what stood out were the photos that line the walls: black-and-white photos of children in overalls standing before a now-forgotten schoolhouse, photos of the old lumber mill before it closed in the late 1980s, photos of long-dead but not forgotten Doverites who made their home on the shores of the river. In one, children are dressed in costumes onstage for a local production. In another, long tables of people enjoy the town's annual picnic, with the church and lake serving as the backdrop. The Dover Girls laugh as they point out their husbands as children in the now eighty-year-old school photos. Old Dover was born again in the photos that had been carefully preserved and captioned.

These photos highlight what was special about Dover to the community. The beauty of the Pend Oreille River and Lake Pend Oreille was never far from their minds, but it mostly served as the background for the relationships that flourished in this place. The bluff, the beach, and the endless fields and forests are meaningful, but primarily because they provided a space to labor and connect meaningfully with the community.

At the entry of the community hall, a birdhouse decorated with ivy and moss serves as a donation box. A cheerful handwritten sign explains: "Donation for Lights & Gas," a reminder that we might not have much, but if we pull together, we still have this place.

Most of the windows in the community hall face old Dover, still looking over the original mill workers' houses and church that were transported upriver in 1922. Slipping into the kitchen and peering out the back window, however, is a reminder of how much Dover has changed. In the 1950s, it would have looked at a tangle of trees, then a deep meadow in the distance, and the community's sandy beach just beyond that. Later, the view would include massive piles of woodchips, the birch trees providing some cover between the building and graying piles of sawdust.

Today, there's a walking path that skirts the back of the community hall and, beyond that, brand-new homes. Dozens of buildings, from condominiums to bungalows to massive mansions, now sit in the fields where the mill once stood. Adorned with natural wood shingles and crisp

I.1. One of the few streets where new homes in the Mill Lake development can be seen in juxtaposition to buildings in the original part of Dover.

white trim, the homes share a similar architectural style, meant to evoke the craftsman style that was popular when the buildings of old Dover were floating up the river. But the homes are unmistakably modern in their attempt to blend the ruggedness of the Pacific Northwest with the comforts of upper-middle-class living.

Lining freshly paved streets, the new homes nestle against the development's headquarters, which features a fitness club and an upscale restaurant. The development was approved in 2004 after a lengthy and contentious struggle with the inhabitants of old Dover. Since then, new Dover has brought waves of new people to the community, drawn by the scenic beauty (and recreational potential) of the river and adjoining lake.

When looking out the window of the old Dover community hall, the new homes are so close, it seems like you might be able to peer inside them. But the new homes are built with their backs to the community center so that they can face the lake and river.

And so it is: old and new, back to back, a path winding between them.

THE WEIGHT OF HISTORY

What brought me back to Dover was not how unusual this bifurcated community is. Rather, it is how typical it is of the changes gripping many rural communities in the United States.

Dover, like almost the entire American West, followed a path that led from the boom of a once-strong timber economy to its bust in the 1980s. Regardless of the industry—timber, mining, or agriculture—nearly all rural communities in the 1980s followed this path. Dover has probably never had more than five hundred residents, but through the 1980s the lumber mill supplied jobs, the town's drinking water, and perhaps most importantly a sense of community and identity. In the 1980s, as the timber industry and extractive industries in the West weakened, the mill in Dover closed, one in a long line of mills that closed in the region. In 1992, after sitting unused for years, the mill burned down, and the community of Dover faced the decision of what would become of their community.

Zoned for agricultural use, the mill site was privately held land. But it was privately held land that for generations had been used by residents of Dover. The mill owners had allowed them to build a baseball diamond, where the Dover River Rats team hosted games. Scores of young mothers had carted children to the beach to learn to swim, one of the last undeveloped natural sandy beaches on the lake. Most of the residents of Dover had never had lakefront views, but they had always had quick access to the lake for swimming, picnicking, fishing, and relaxing. The mill workers' homes were built in tidy rows a mile from the mill, sitting far back from the water to ensure they didn't flood in the days before a dam was built downriver.

In 2004, the Dover City Council voted 3–1 to approve a 600-unit upscale development, forever altering their community and transitioning the once-bustling lumber mill town into a destination for retirees and outdoor enthusiasts. The development branded itself "Mill Lake" (a pseudonym) and included plenty of opportunities for recreation for those with money. There's a huge marina that juts into the lake, where people can dock their boats or even their floatplanes. Helicopter parking is, of course, also available. There is a restaurant and a fitness club with a pool. There are fountains and statues. There's even a branded, oversized Adirondack chair where visitors are encouraged to pose with all their friends and then share on social media how carefree Mill Lake has made them.

But mostly there are houses and condos and bungalows. On its website, Mill Lake bills itself as a "master planned waterfront community with 14 different neighborhoods." Each neighborhood is outlined on the map of the development, with names like "Marina Tower" and "Reedwalk." The map is drawn so that the opposite shore of the Pend Oreille River is eliminated, and the river is renamed "Lake Pend Oreille." It is as if the development exists in a different world, where the rules of naming bodies of water are more like guidelines.

Mill Lake is a simulacrum for an American West that never existed. It features reproductions of old-timey street lamps that line the tree-edged boulevard into Mill Lake. There are no streetlights at all in old Dover.

What happened in Dover is a common story in communities across the American West, especially in those "lucky" enough to be situated against scenic landscapes, ripe for tourism and outdoor recreation. As extractive industries such as timber, mining, or agriculture faltered in an era of automation and globalization, the dwindling remnants of communities that had relied on those industries were "saved" by new developments promising more people and the return of steady employment. Sitting on the edge of a river ringed by mountains in every direction, with bald eagles nesting on the riverbank, Dover was a prime target for developers who might have peppered the shore with megamansions or gated off the land to the whole community. Now the material extracted from the region is the cheap labor of those left behind to staff the restaurants, marinas, ski lifts, and coffee shops.

Of course, most communities have very little say in what becomes of them, but Dover, because of decisions made years earlier, seemed to maintain some power. The city council could have used zoning regulations to control the mill site and stop any new developments in their community. And the decision to allow the development was controversial, given the dramatic changes the new construction would bring. "Decision

Inspires Both Delight and Horror" was the headline story for September 4, 2004, in the *Bonner County Daily Bee*, after the council finally voted to rezone the land. According to the article, opponents of the development were "moved to tears," while another was "inspired to rip to shreds a stack of pamphlets touting [Mill Lake]" during the meeting.[1]

So why did the council approve the development? Dover was hardly thriving in the decades after the lumber mill closed and then later burned to the ground, but the community maintained a stubborn pride in its autonomy, resisting annexation from nearby Sandpoint and clinging to its identity. What would lead this tight-knit community to so radically alter their beloved town?

When I started my research, I had assumed that the Dover Girls would have led the charge against the Mill Lake development given their attachment to old Dover and long history in the town. After all, they seemed to have significant power over the process: the city council that approved it was made up of their blue-collar and pink-collar friends, family, and neighbors. But while the women dutifully attended the town meetings concerning the development, they sat toward the back. As others in the community led efforts to derail the planned development, the Dover Girls bore witness but maintained their silence.

I struggled at first to understand how these unabashedly outspoken women who obviously held significant sway in the community didn't do more to stop the development. But as I got to know them, surrounded by the photos of their past and their stories of Dover's glory days, their reluctance to get involved came into focus. As I learned about the history of Dover and the decades-long struggles of the town to keep the community together, I came to a similar conclusion as had the Dover Girls. The history of Dover had taught them that, for working-class people like themselves, these kinds of decisions were largely beyond their control.

As the story of Dover unfolded before me, I began to realize that the history of the development was written a century before it was built. On the surface, it was the people of Dover who decided the fate of the old mill site and whether it would or would not be rezoned. But once you step back from that city council vote to see the longer historical trajectory, it becomes only one in a long series of decisions and policies that led to the new Dover. The story of that vote is not just the story of a new development but also one of an aging infrastructure that left an already economically depressed community constantly in the red. It is the story of a community struggling to get the owners of the mill site to take any kind of responsibility for the fate of the town and to recognize the community's rights. And, looking even further back, it is the story of railroad barons and timber tycoons who made their riches off stolen lands only to leave a legacy of neglect and inequity in the communities they helped to create.

This book outlines the history that led to the development by exploring the forces that shaped that pivotal vote, in which the city council members seemingly voted against their interests. Voting in favor of the development would mean losing access to most of the communal spaces that had been vital to old Dover: the beach, bluff, and baseball field. The development offered little hope that existing homes would increase in value, nor did the old-timers in Dover imagine children returning home, able to afford one of the new homes in the development. And yet the city council and the old-timers ultimately supported the development, bowing to the historical forces privileging those with money and power to shape the American West as they see fit.

In the intervening years since the newspaper described the decidedly mixed reaction to the development, Dover has been radically altered. The sandy beach where generations of residents swam sat behind a "no trespassing" sign for a decade; now an enormous home occupies the space. The residents of old Dover wait and debate about how big the lakefront homes that eventually will block their view of the old beach should be. The developer, by contrast, points to the new public beach he built for the community (complete with bathrooms), the new open-beamed city hall that he donated to the city, and the miles of public paths. A few of the old-timers have taken the liberty of naming the new public beach "Goose-Shit Beach" and cannot help but point out that the developer built it on the river, not the lake. Rather than the soft sloping sand of the old beach, the new one is rocky and steep. It is also as far from old Dover as possible.

Many of those who were the most upset about the development have attempted to let it go. One resident of old Dover burned a decade-old box of letters to the editor, reports, and clippings that were beginning to feel like an albatross. Some moved, unable to watch the transition without feeling a constant and profound sense of loss. Many of those who were ambivalent or even supportive of the development now say they feel tricked by it. Many of the promises they claim the developer made—like being able to launch fishing boats for free—failed to materialize. And so, even years later the development continues to cause both delight and horror.

METHODS

When I started this project, I primarily wanted to understand why Dover was developed. I thought the answer might be simple, but I found that each answer brought a new set of questions. This book, therefore, is a case study that pulls together information and data from many sources. The first stage of the project took nearly a year and involved interviews with over thirty people. I interviewed residents who lived in new apartments in the development and the man who planned where that apartment building should sit. Next, I interviewed the man who surveyed the wetlands so the developer could decide where to place that apartment building. Then I interviewed the opponents to the development, who worked tirelessly to convince the city council that the wetlands were too valuable to allow development on them. I also interviewed the man who designed the new sewer system, and the daughter of the man who spent Christmas Eve trying to get the old water system to work. I interviewed residents who had worked in the mill, who had been born in the mill workers' houses, and who arrived by wagon to the shores of Lake Pend Oreille. I interviewed mayors and city councilors and newcomers who had retired after years of public service to spend their final decades in a modest apartment or home in the new Mill Lake development.

Every interview was fully transcribed and then coded, meaning that I highlighted them line by line, recording the themes in each line. By the end of the project, I generated nearly 175 separate codes; each interview was broken into pieces organized by idea into these categories. I quit conducting interviews only after they started sounding very familiar and were no longer generating new codes. This is a positive sign in social science research that I had reached "saturation," a point in the process where I was no longer learning something new and that I was confident that I had effectively learned what there was to know about the question I had posed.

I am deeply grateful to the folks who shared their time with me, who welcomed me into their homes and offices, who poured me cups of hot coffee and allowed themselves to be vulnerable to my endless curiosity about their lives and roles in Dover. My research followed the legal and ethical guidelines set forth by the University of Idaho's Office of Institutional Research and my professional responsibilities as outlined by the American Sociological Association, including using pseudonyms for all individuals I interviewed.

It is here where I apologize. Many of the people I interviewed preferred to be acknowledged by name in this book. And for quite some time I imagined doing so. However, the convention in sociological research is to use pseudonyms to protect those who participate. Our research should do no harm to the individuals involved. Using real names meant bucking established norms, and thus I would need to be able to make a strong case about why I decided to name my participants. In the end, I did not feel that I could make that case. Ultimately what led me to decide to give all participants pseudonyms is that some, for professional and personal reasons, only agreed to be interviewed if those interviews were kept confidential. It became increasingly difficult to keep some respondents confidential, as they requested, and to name others, because it's a small community and interviewees often referenced each other. I could not effectively discuss these social networks and also keep key people's identities confidential.

That said, I struggled with my decision, because many participants, particularly those whose families were some of the first settlers in the area, were anxious to participate precisely so they could share their (often incredible) family legacies. In a county where certain last names hold inordinate sway, this project offered an opportunity to disrupt the power of those supposedly important names by naming those who did extraordinary things in the everyday business of building a life for the generations that came after them. I was touched by the warmth and generosity of these families. These are the names that should be revered in our history books, those who do the right thing even when no one is looking. I also realize that they will likely be the first to offer forgiveness that I may not deserve. This was a decision that kept me up at night but one I ultimately believe to be the one I was professionally and ethically bound to make.

My search also included significant archival work at the Bonner County Historical Society, where I was given access to old newspaper articles, historical photos, and other documents. This historical work, however, would have been significantly harder if not for an unofficial historian of Dover who neatly organized binders full of materials—historical newspapers and decades-old personal correspondence, such as letters and bills—that were instrumental in creating a timeline for understanding Dover's water woes.

My research also involved many hours at Dover City Hall, poring over the notes from city council meetings and hearings. It was the Dover city clerk who carefully pulled file after file from storage, revealing records that hadn't seen the light of day for decades. And it was the same city clerk who seemed even more shocked than I was when important documents were simply missing from the files and the audiotape backups for those events, carefully organized in a big box labeled "Mill Lake Development," were blank—all twenty-six of them.

Ultimately, my goal as a researcher is to triangulate my data, in other words, to make certain that all the data points in this book reinforce each other in order to draw conclusions. At times, this meant searching out additional data using the Freedom of Information Act and public records requests to verify and clarify my interview data. Specifically, I requested documents from the Army Corps of Engineers and the Idaho State Historic Preservation Office.

All these documents and interviews were used to create various timelines of events for significant occurrences in Dover. After I had done so, I then overlaid them with the larger historical context of that period. My interview data and other primary source data were woven together with a variety of secondary sources, such as books, articles, websites, and reports. These secondary sources fleshed out the particular history of Dover by contextualizing it within other histories that structured the community; these include histories of the Kalispel people, with help from the Kalispel Tribe of Indians' cultural resource manager, Kevin Lyons. Other important works included Nancy Foster Renk's book on the Humbird Lumber Company in Sandpoint, *A Glorious Field for Sawmills.*

Her work was essential to understanding the role of sawmills in North Idaho, the American frontier, and the railroad industry. Weaving together these histories with a theoretical paradigm that explores the social structures that organized them, this project then broadly explains the conditions that made Dover ripe for development while simultaneously laying out the very specific conditions there.

THEORIZING DOVER'S DEVELOPMENT

The city council's decision to approve the development and the long history leading up to that decision serve as an illustrative case study of change in rural communities. One of the ways scholars have understood this change is through the lens of what has been termed "rural gentrification," or the in-migration of more affluent urban and suburban populations into rural areas, drawn there by the charm of rural communities, the scenic beauty of rural spaces, and the lower cost of living. Rural gentrification has become a key concept in analyzing the declining fortunes of some rural communities and the possible solutions to rural economic stagnation.[2] However, the prospect of urbanites and suburbanites who are more affluent leveraging their relative wealth and transforming working-class, rural areas raises questions about cultural and economic power and the autonomy of rural communities.[3]

The complexities of rural gentrification are often obscured by popular press accounts of rural communities as universally in decline, as seen in news reports like a recent *New York Times* article titled "Small-Town America Is Dying," wherein the reporter laments "America's languishing rural communities."[4] The reality, however, is far more complex for rural communities in the United States. USDA researcher Lorin Kusmin notes that, while "the population of rural America has declined by 116,000 over the last 4 years," these overall losses are overshadowed by big population gains in certain rural locations: "These counties are concentrated in scenic areas such as the Rocky Mountains or southern Appalachia."[5]

While some rural communities are losing population and suffer from chronic poverty, others have become popular destinations for in-migrants, thanks to the economic opportunities of the energy boom or the draw of rural lifestyles. This "amenity migration" (a "movement of people based on the draw of natural and/or cultural amenities"[6]) draws new residents to the scenic beauty of the areas. Specifically, amenity migration refers to "the purchasing of primary or second residences in rural areas valued for their aesthetic, recreational, and other consumption-orientated use-values."[7] As part of this amenity migration, new arrivals bring with them cultural and economic power that outweighs that of current residents, which often radically alters the communities these amenity migrants move to.

The works of J. Dwight Hines (2010) and Rina Ghose (2004) suggest that this process is particularly pronounced in the American West, and use the term *rural gentrification* to understand it.[8] In the American West, rural gentrification is a result of a desire for a "celebrated Rocky Mountain lifestyle" but with expectations of "certain urban amenities such as good community infrastructure, cultural activities and a variety of shopping and dining opportunities."[9] For Ghose, rural gentrification, like urban gentrification, is about the "commodification of space and displacement of residents."[10]

Rural gentrification, then, is becoming an increasingly important concept in theories about the bifurcated population growth of the rural United States. Requiring both (1) a demographic shift of populations from urban and suburban areas to rural ones, according to particular timelines and in particular locations, and (2) the influx of a population with social and economic power to rural areas where they can assert that power,[11] rural gentrification today can be understood as the "colonization of rural communities and small-towns by members of the ex-urban middle class."[12]

Communities that survived the shift away from extractive industries, then, did so by following this model, turning to tourists, many of whom became residents. While many others in North Idaho and the Mountain West have struggled, communities like Dover (and its larger neighbors Sandpoint and Coeur d'Alene) have been able to use the lure of picturesque mountain lakes to transition into tourism- or service-based economies. Even if these in-migrants change the towns they enter, the resulting population gains are often celebrated as reinvigorating rural communities, bringing people and jobs to areas hit hard by the decline in extractive industries.

But for many communities in the Rocky Mountains, the relationship between population and jobs is fraught. This transition does not necessarily mean the kinds of stable career opportunities that extractive industries created in the recent past. An influx of people, drawn by the scenic beauty, may well create jobs in their new communities, but most often these are low-paying service-sector jobs, while at the same time, the cost of living, particularly in housing, often rapidly increases. So while new populations—whether temporary or permanent—increase the overall population, good-paying, stable jobs might still leave these towns.

In this way, rural gentrification has real consequences for the people and places impacted by these demographic changes. These include the displacement of poor, working-class, and middle-class people from areas experiencing gentrification because of the increasing price of housing and land, sometimes pushing existing residents into communities that are considered "chronically poor," where they can afford housing.[13] Thus, these demands create new opportunities and tensions within the community, particularly its land-use patterns.

Local residents who are not physically displaced, however, risk being culturally displaced. As Paul Cloke and Jo Little note, the unequal cultural power brought with gentrifiers enables them to "impose a degree of social and cultural hegemony over consumption choices" and, in doing so, to impose quite profound changes on the social and physical environment.[14]

Yet, while the changes wrought by rural gentrification are widely acknowledged, much of the research around it "has centered on migrants themselves (the demand side), [and thus] we know far less about the influence of other social actors. Real estate developers, neighbouring and exiting agricultural and forestry producers, third-party property managers, renters, and others play key roles in mediating between the actual or perceived motivations of amenity migrants and resulting ecological dynamics."[15]

It is true that when researchers try to make sense of change in rural communities they often focus on the newcomers: their identity formation, their consumption patterns, and the cultural and economic pull factors that led them to migrate.[16] However, by focusing on the amenity migrants themselves, rural gentrification can seem like it is the result of individual choices, rather than the structures, policies, and histories that have laid a foundation for this kind of wholesale change.

This book takes a different approach to understanding rural gentrification. In the chapters that follow, I contextualize the changes in Dover by situating its story within a conversation about the broad economic, social, and political forces that have shaped the landscape of this community. I argue that rural gentrification is not simply about the choices of in-migrants or even developers but part of an expansive pattern involving a host of social actors embedded within particular histories and economic structures.

In "Writing the New West," the authors note, "We believe that if researchers reconceptualize the West as part of a larger political, cultural, and ecological transition, not only can practical lessons be derived from previously overlooked sites (both within the United States and around the world) but insights emerging from research on the U.S. West will inform research in other places."[17] This book, then, centers the "political, cultural, and ecological transition" in Dover to understand the macrolevel histories and processes that inform the transformation of the West.

Throughout, I use a historical material perspective to delve into the details of people's everyday lives and use them to understand what happened in Dover. I use the historical record to connect people's private struggles—the closing of mills, for example—to the larger history of the area. C. Wright Mills calls this connecting of personal problems to public issues "the sociological imagination." Using primary and secondary source materials, this book uses the sociological imagination to connect the historical record from both the turn of the twentieth century and from the 1980s to the lives of individuals in Dover in these periods.

Following the lead of other scholars, I use David Harvey's theory of "the spatial fix" to contextualize the global economic forces that the people of Dover experienced, to understand these public issues in Dover.[18] Drawing heavily from Marxian theory, Harvey's spatial fix explains the realities of globalization. Focusing on the importance of space and temporality to globalization, Harvey notes that capitalism must be geographically expansive over time in order to outrun the inherent crisis of overaccumulation. His concept of a spatial fix suggests a cyclical process that uses time and space to manage the crises of capitalism—the boom-and-bust cycles—that we have been asked to accept as normal.

According to Harvey, the first step of the spatial fix requires what Marx might call primitive accumulation. Harvey suggests that before capitalism can become viable, it "has to build a fixed space (or 'land-scape') necessary for its own functioning at a certain point in its history."[19] Looking historically, Marx argued that this process happened in England with the advent of the enclosure laws, which were written to push peasants off commonly held grazing, growing, and hunting lands and into cities like London, where their labor was the necessary fuel for the growing industrial revolution. This pushing of people off the land and into factories happened at the same time that colonial powers were accumulating riches using barbarous violence in Africa and the Americas. This is all to say that capitalism is not some natural system that simply emerges from some primordial soup. Instead, it requires the class of people who will profit from the labor of others to build a place where this system can thrive. It also requires organizing the political and social systems that support this economic arrangement for the benefit of this class.

Harvey argues that building a space for capitalism, while necessary in the first stage, later becomes a barrier to profit as the market shifts—and it always shifts: wages are lower elsewhere, or a new factory located a thousand miles away is more efficient, and the fixed cost of whatever was built earlier remains sunk in that original landscape. Thus, to once again create profit, the capitalists must "destroy that space [they built] (and devalue much of the capital invested therein) at a later point."[20]

The exhaustion of resources within the landscape of capitalism requires a spatial fix or the creation of "openings for fresh accumulation in new spaces and territories."[21] As a result, Harvey argues, "capitalism could not survive without being geographically expansionary (and perpetually seeking out 'spatial fixes' for its problems)."[22] Capitalism as an economic system destroys spaces and people and must then move to new spaces to find workers, resources, and landscapes to exploit. This expansion then necessitates new spatial fixes and new organizations of labor and resources.

The concept of the spatial fix allows us to situate the process of rural gentrification in a larger context that speaks to the histories of power and exploitation of capitalism. Thus, rural gentrification should be seen not as a new phenomenon but rather the expected outcome of a social system that privileges the economic growth of the few over other ways of organizing social life.

This book applies the process of the spatial fix to Dover. Simplified, the spatial fix can be understood as follows: first, create a space for capitalism; later, destroy that space when it is no longer profitable; finally, return and reorganize that space in order to once again maximize profit there.

The building of a space for capitalism in Dover is quite clear. Dover exists because building a railroad and mills created unimaginable wealth for a handful of men who were sold huge tracts of land, which the state had taken by force from Indigenous people, in exchange for a pittance. The creation of this wealth is situated against the backdrop of the forced removal of the Kalispel people and then the exploitation of the labor of the people who built the railroad and felled the timber. However, rather than simply seeing the process of building a space for capitalism as a literal process of erecting buildings and bridges, throughout the book, I suggest that we understand it as a process of simultaneously building the political and social systems that support the interests of those who build a space for capitalism, in the case of Dover, the mill owners and later the developer.

Discussing the next phase of the spatial fix—the destruction of space— I highlight how the loss of the mill and the jobs it provided combined with decaying infrastructure to set the stage for Dover to be rezoned for development. While the role destruction plays in Dover's subsequent development is quite literal in many of the examples from this community, my research suggests that the process of destroying a space extends well beyond a mill burning or a sewer system being red-tagged. Instead, it is also about the destruction of solidarities among community members, as well as the destruction of people's belief that they should get a say in the future of their space.

Finally, I turn to the last stage of the spatial fix by examining Dover after the Mill Lake development is built. This section examines how the process of rebuilding a space for capitalism means not only the building of houses and marinas but also a system of regulations and ordinances that organize the community around the economic interests of the developer and the residents of Mill Lake. It also asks us to consider what it means to build communities around the profit motive of developers rather than the many other social, spiritual, and economic needs of people and their communities.

This book highlights that the choices of individuals do not exist in a vacuum. The framework of the spatial fix contextualizes the contemporary question of rural gentrification within longer histories that explain these migration patterns. Rural gentrification, according to this logic, is not a new phenomenon but rather an expected outcome of the routine functions of capitalism in these rural spaces.

Too often, the inequalities that result from development are dismissed as the "natural" outcome of progress or growth. But the processes that led to a development like Mill Lake are anything but "natural." A long history of exploitation, coupled with a legal and political system that privileges the rights of property owners over communities, has shaped Dover as a town since its inception. The path to development was determined by the same political and economic forces that placed Dover on the banks of the river over a hundred years ago.

Of course, these political and economic forces are sometimes obscured as people look for scapegoats who can be vilified for seeking profits over the well-being of communities. For many communities, including Dover, the specter of the greedy developer fills this role, as the community blames bad actors in the process. The reorganization of rural spaces thanks to development, however, is not simply the result of a set of bad actors who take pleasure in others' suffering. Instead, it is the expected outcome of laws and policies that make what may not be ethical perfectly legal. Developers are only playing one role in the expansive project of rural gentrification, a process resulting from laws, policies, and economic structures, not simply individual actors.

Too often in struggling rural communities, any capital returning to them is perceived as positive. Communities are expected to applaud every dollar that comes their way. The dollars that may or may not find their way to rural communities as a result of development, however, are not the primary outcome of developments like Mill Lake. Instead, these developments restructure rural spaces to make them profitable for those with capital. Any economic benefits for the existing community are tangential to the spatial and economic project of rural development. In this way, we should never assume that development is a process that will lift all boats or function to rejuvenate rural communities.

As a result of these processes, we end up with communities that are deeply divided by social and economic class, often literally, as old-timers and newcomers see the idea of community, space, and the environment so differently. Class differences in gentrified rural communities such as Dover yield very different perspectives on space and nature, from how wilderness should be appreciated to the utility of property ownership. Is a river for fishing or kayaking? Are the woods for hiking or ATVing? Is one's yard for natural beauty or overflow storage from one's garage? These cultural assumptions around space are built into new developments and new communities, creating tensions and separating community members by social class.

In this way, what is called the new American West, like the old American West, is defined by conflict and competing visions of space. By understanding the historical process that led us from the Old West to this New West, we can attempt to imagine an alternative West, neither old or nor new, that seeks to integrate rather than divide communities.

The name scholars give these phenomena or the theories that explain them—rural gentrification, amenity migration, the spatial fix—provide a shorthand for discussing complex ideas. But these terms can sometimes end up flattening the complexity of lives involved. My work here attempts to add nuance to our understanding of change in the rural West. I hope to contextualize how the people living in these changing communities understand and experience that change.

This book, then, is a case study of a particular instance of change in a rural community and the cast of characters involved in this change, who each provide a portrait of the Old and New West. The old mayor of Dover, Marty Jones, for example, is a retired union railroad worker who oversaw decisions about the development. He raises livestock and favors dirty coveralls and a cowboy hat. His successor, Kate Morris, is busy raising children in a lakefront house in the Mill Lake development. Mayor Morris's house is built on the bluff, where Jones's wife grew up riding her horses.

Whether we understand their roles in the story of Dover through the lens of rural gentrification or the New versus Old West or the "spatial fix," this book tells the story of real people whose lives illustrate a complex social and political history.

The story of Dover is both a universal one about the changes in the rural West and particular to this community. It's the story of missing city council minutes and blank tapes—including all the records and tapes of the fateful "delight and horror" public meeting. Depending on whom you ask, it is the story of a "local boy" making good by developing Dover and keeping it open to the public—or a bully who threatened anyone who opposed him and then reneged on the promises he made to the locals. Dover is the story of the rural West, where survival for working-class people once meant logging or agriculture and now means building homes or waiting tables and being grateful that you have a house to build or table to wait on because it means your community is still there.

Dover, in other words, can tell us a very specific story about particular people struggling to hold their town together, but it also tells an expansive tale about changes in the American West driven by economic, environmental, and political pressures to "fix" the problems that capitalism itself created.

THE CHAPTERS

Using interviews with the Idaho state geologist and the cultural resource manager for the Kalispel nation in addition to archived regional newspapers, chapter 1, "A Brief History of the Last 62 Million Years," situates the mill site in Dover within a broad historical context. Drawing out an expansive historical narrative about geological change and land use in the rural West, it explores the long history that led to the formation of a mill in Dover in 1907. This history spans the long-standing and continued relationship of the land to the Kalispel nation, to the coming of the railroads and lumber barons, and to the key labor disputes that brought the Industrial Workers of the World (IWW) to the community to demand an eight-hour workday.

This chapter argues that the opening of Indigenous peoples' lands in the West to extractive industries was not to create prosperity for settlers, nor was it intended to offer long-term prosperity for rural communities. Instead, the white settlement was designed to enrich timber and railroad barons by building a space for capitalism, ultimately leaving rural communities like Dover vulnerable, since they were not designed for the long-term health of the settlers who were lured by the promise of work and land.

Chapter 2, "Water, Water, Everywhere," continues this historical narrative into the 1980s, beginning with a letter that Dover residents received informing them that the mill, which had provided drinking water since its inception, would "cease from supplying water to non-company owned properties." In essence, the community of five hundred people would be left without drinkable water. Using interviews, archival data, and city records, the chapter details the six long years the people of Dover lived under a boil order. At the same time, Dover dealt with constant job insecurity: the mill would open and close sporadically as the timber industry in North Idaho increased the amount of lumber produced while simultaneously decreasing the number of workers as a result of automation and consolidation.

Chapter 2, then, explores the role that declining infrastructure plays in debates around rural gentrification, exploring the structural preconditions for "destruction" that would eventually lead the community to open the door to development.

The city of Dover was nearly destroyed by a fire in 1990 when the mill burned to the ground, leading to yet another failing-infrastructure issue plaguing the community: the sewer system. Tying together the closing and burning of the mill with the dire situation of the town's sewers, chapter 3, "Shit Rolls Downhill," carefully illustrates how the mill's owners abdicated responsibility for the deteriorating infrastructure in Dover while simultaneously using the deep vulnerabilities created by this situation to demand that the city rezone their property. The subsequent zoning change from agriculture to planned use development would eventually allow the mill's owners to sell the property at a huge profit.

Chapter 3 continues chapter 2's discussion of failing infrastructure as a formative stage in the process of rural gentrification. This chapter especially explores the power the mill owners turned developers deployed in facilitating and then profiting from the neglected community infrastructure.

Chapter 4, "It's ~~Not~~ Over in Dover," explains how residents attempted to stop the development, as well as the ecological frame they used to try to motivate their neighbors, while highlighting how this frame was ultimately ineffective at creating a broader network of opposition, in part because some residents believed that the mill site was too polluted to be considered ecologically important. Those same residents also believed that it was an ecological frame that shuttered the mill in the first place. Finally, the chapter discusses how the opposition to the development often cast the developer himself as a bad actor rather than fully addressing the failures of political and state regulators.

Chapter 4 explores the challenges of organizing against development in rural communities and argues that the demonization of "environmentalists" in timber communities is designed to distract from the material reality: that mills are quite successful in the region but their former workers are not. This chapter argues that, ultimately, the building of a space for capitalism is about building a network of bureaucracies and ideologies designed for the construction of developments, rather than resisting them, and shows that the demonization of "developers" may distract from the system of laws that hands power to those developers rather than to communities.

While many longtime residents did not oppose the development for a variety of reasons, they did have a long history of agitating against the mill site owners. Using interviews and archival data, chapter 5, "Anarchists on the Beach," discusses the numerous fights these residents had with the mill owners and then developers to preserve their access to their community spaces. These efforts included teens setting traps on the beach to try to thwart the landowners' caretaker, which ends up with a boy being hit over the head with a pipe by said caretaker. The chapter discusses how losing this fight year after year left the residents feeling powerless against the mill owners, explaining why they ultimately decided to make a fragile allegiance with the "local boy" developer whom they hoped would do right by them.

Chapter 5 continues the argument in chapter 4 by focusing on the reasons that many community members chose not to fight the development and instead decided their only hope in keeping Dover an open community was to work with the "local" developer. This chapter argues that the "old-timers" used the only power they felt they had—social networks—to keep Dover from becoming a gated community. It also highlights the consequences of the destruction of not just the buildings in Dover but also community solidarities.

The next chapter moves on to discuss the development. Detailing and describing the amenities of Mill Lake, chapter 6, "A Mill Lake Moment," examines how the development was organized around the imagined desires of the new residents it hoped to attract. From the fitness center and the marina to the dog park and the restaurant, this chapter explores how amenity migration shaped Mill Lake. It applies the various taxonomies scholars use to describe the American West and the rural United States more generally—"booming, bypassed, and protected West" and "the New and Old West"—to North Idaho and Dover in particular, while examining the impact on working-class communities when they are pushed out of conversations about how the land can or should be used.

This chapter asks the reader to consider how what is constructed as "environmentally sensitive" is tied to social class, as well as how terms like the "booming" and "bypassed" West have the potential to normalize rural gentrification as simply the natural order of the West. This chapter suggests that gentrification be understood as the outcome of particular power relations. It shows that building a space for capitalism that centers profit, rather than the needs of people in those communities, makes it difficult for people to connect across class and other divisions.

Chapter 7, "A Tale of Two Dovers," describes the two communities that have formed in the ten years since the development was approved—old Dover and Mill Lake—and the challenges of creating a single community. Instead of measuring the impacts of rural gentrification only by looking at population increases and job growth, this chapter explores the failures of community cohesion between the two Dovers that emerged in the wake of the development. It describes how longtime residents have adjusted to the development and the challenges they face in maintaining community as they watch their children and grandchildren leave to find work and affordable housing in the region.

These debates about newcomers and fractured communities are often taken up in scholarly discussions of gentrification and its effects, but this chapter suggests that the building of developments is also about the building of political, economic, and social systems that privilege an upper-class perspective. I highlight several small changes—such as leash laws and a new city ordinance that bans junk—as examples of how class inequality is being amplified in Dover and how they exacerbate the class barriers between the two Dovers. This chapter, then, demonstrates how class dynamics play out in the processes of rural gentrification and the unique class distinctions of the rural American West.

Tying together the previous chapters, the conclusion, "Everything That's Old Is New Again," shows that what we see in Dover exemplifies David Harvey's vision of a "spatial fix" for capitalism. The historical processes that led to the Mill Lake development were not a "natural" consequence of progress but rather the result of a clear system privileging those with wealth and property in the American West. This is not to say that working-class communities didn't find a way to organize themselves to meet their interests, but the political and economic structures were not designed for the prosperity or autonomy of the people who felled the trees. Those structures were designed by and for the people who owned the timberland and the rail lines to haul that timber. The mechanisms that enabled the Mill Lake development were simply a continuation of this logic, as those with power allowed the town to deteriorate to the point that development seemed to be the only option for the community.

To demonstrate that this was not the only possible outcome for towns like Dover, I also imagine what alternatives to development might have looked like. Drawing examples from other communities that have pushed back against development, I outline some possible visions of Dover that could have rejected the logic of development. In this way, I hope to remind us that the future of our communities is being written by what we do today.

1

A Brief History of the Last 62 Million Years

THE BLUFF IS a beacon, lofting 145 feet above the surface of the lake and marking the source of the Pend Oreille River as it flows from Lake Pend Oreille. It is almost perfectly round, a dome of granite rising from the water. In the spring, it is covered in camas flowers and shaded by soaring evergreens. The base of the bluff is punctuated by smaller boulders that peek out of the water's edge, perfect for sunbathing and diving. At the northern edge of the bluff sits a stretch of sandy beach, the beach that generations of Dover residents used as the local swimming spot.

The bluff and the watershed around it are the historic homeland of the Kalispel people, who navigated the Pend Oreille River—and the many lakes, rivers, and streams that connect the watershed—in their sturgeon-nosed canoes. Their relationship with the waters of this place can be understood in the details of their lives. The canoes are drawn into narrow points that skirt the surface at both ends so they can navigate the reeds and winds of the region. Their canoes are so specialized to this place that only "two other tribes in the world used this type of canoe."[1] Because of their design, they are light enough to be carried by a single person but able to carry entire families. The juxtaposition of something so light carrying so much weight meant that oral histories from early white settlers to the region make frequent mention of the Kalispel people's skills at canoe engineering.

Today, the river and lake are used for very different purposes; they are now crisscrossed by motorboats and jet skis. And rather than towering over forests and wetlands, the bluff overlooks a burgeoning network of lakeside condos. Over the centuries, it has been a silent witness to a host of changes.

When I would tell people about the story of Dover, Idaho, of how a sleepy mill town became an upscale development, it was not uncommon to be met with a sigh and then a statement about how you can't stop progress. For most people, change is simply inevitable, like erosion or the changing of the seasons. And certainly, the story of this space, this wide expanse of water scooped and deposited here by glaciers, is the story of change. No space stays as it was for all time, but the scope of the change Dover has experienced in only the last seven generations—the last 140 years—is not a result of the laws of physics. What happened in Dover was not inevitable. Instead, it is the result of an economic and political arrangement that used Dover as it used much of the American West (and other settler-colonial spaces): to extract profit from the land at the expense of people and the land itself. It is irresponsible to conflate the inevitability and pace of geological change with changes wrought through particular arrangements of capital and political power.

This chapter, then, charts the long history of Dover before the 1980s, telling the history of a space whose uses and meanings have been radically transformed over the past century and a half. From the Kalispel people's vision of stewardship to the massive projects of extraction spearheaded by timber barons to the struggles of workers to build sustainable lives and communities, Dover, like the rest of the Pacific Northwest, has been a constant site of turmoil and transformation since the arrival of white settlers.

This history illustrates how a landscape for capitalism was built starting in the late 1880s as capitalist interests began to reshape the West (literally and figuratively).[2] The landscape that was built is not the result of a "natural" or inevitable process in which the West was settled by plucky, hardworking Americans. Rather, it was a deliberate process in which state and private interests instituted new structures of land ownership and labor relations that maximized their profitability. The settlement of the West is often romanticized as the work of rugged individuals seeking new lives in new spaces, but the history of Dover shows how this new landscape was constructed according to the spatial and capitalist logics of railroad and timber barons, with Indigenous people, settlers, and laborers always struggling to assert their autonomy and dignity in the process.

Rather than demonstrating the inevitability of change, these transformations reveal a series of strategic policies and economic structures that systematically eroded the opportunities for everyday people in the American West to shape their destinies.

DEEP TIME AND THE KALISPEL PEOPLE

Of course, the area around what would eventually become Dover has experienced changes over the great expanse of geological time. There have been volcanic eruptions, ice ages, and floods of biblical proportions that shaped the land. Geologists say that the bluff was created forty-eight million years old ago, deep underground, when the land experienced violent volcanic eruptions and lava flows. When trapped underground, the lava cooled slowly and crystalized into granite. For millions of years, this base of rock was hidden beneath a layer of sedimentary rock. The bluff only emerged as the sedimentary layer above it, the Belt Supergroup, eroded. Geologists believe it took millions of years for this slow revelation of the bluff's granite.[3]

The scars on the mountains that ring Lake Pend Oreille tell a story about the process of that creation. During the last ice age, the bluff sat buried in mile-thick glaciers. The bluff sits only thirty miles from the edge of a glacial dam that held back a 3,000-square-mile lake—a body of water bigger than several of the Great Lakes combined. The bluff would have been one of the first witnesses to the Glacial Lake Missoula floods, which are credited with creating the scablands of Eastern Washington, leaving giant boulders and dry waterfalls in the middle of a desert. It would have seen this ice dam failing and the sixteen cubic miles of water an hour that hemorrhaged out. Geologists estimate that the water would have rushed out for a week and covered over a 16,000-square-mile area in Montana, Idaho, Washington, and Oregon.[4] Happening over and over again for thousands of years, the floods deposited clay, silt, and sand, slowly filling in the area around and behind the bluff until it was connected, however tenuously, to the land.

For the Kalispel people, the ever-changing contours of the lake and river have always been their home, even as the waters rose and fell from season to season and from year to year. While beliefs about what created the world are as varied as the people who tell them, one Salish Culture Committee story tells that the Creator sent Coyote and his brother, Fox, to make the world, this big island for the people, to free it from evils, and to create the landscape.[5] This story is about change too, a world before humans walked the earth and the world after.

Archaeologists suggest that humans have called the Pend Oreille River valley home for the last 8,000–10,000 years.[6] The Kalispel people who did so were organized into two groups, the Upper Kalispel bands (who are now most often called the Pend Oreille) and the Lower Kalispel bands (now more commonly known as the Kalispel tribe). The traditional homeland of the Kalispel people stretched north to Priest Lake, west into what is now Washington, and east into Montana, following the lakes and rivers that eventually spill into the mighty Columbia River. The miles of river along the outlet of Lake Pend Oreille, including Dover, mark a shared space between the groups.[7]

Today the Kalispel and Pend Oreille tribal centers are spread across different reservations: many Pend Oreille people were forced onto the Flathead Indian Reservation in Western Montana in the 1880s along with people from the Bitterroot Salish and Kootenai tribes; "the lower Kalispel bands," on the other hand, "doggedly resisted resettlement only to eventually realize their own reservation by 1914."[8] When Native peoples were forced onto reservations, there was no attempt to keep tribal communities intact. If you happened to be hunting bison in Montana or celebrating with neighbors to the south when the US military was rounding up Indigenous people, that's where you ended up—away from your homeland and away from your family. Thus, today the Kalispel people's lives are centered around reservations in Montana and Washington, when much of their traditional homeland is in Idaho.

Archaeological records suggest that the Kalispel people relied on fish from these waters to feed their community for thousands of years. By following the spawning schedule of each fish—the bull trout, westslope cutthroat trout, and mountain whitefish—the Kalispel had a predictable food source. While their neighbors to the west relied on salmon and their neighbors to the east relied on bison, the Kalispel lived off the bounty that was unique to this place. In a region where snow can blanket the valleys in October and stay through April or even May, the people spent a great deal of time preparing stocks of food for the winter months. The Kalispel were also considered extraordinary hunters and relied upon hunting deer, in particular, to feed themselves throughout the long winters. Kevin Lyons, the cultural resource manager for the Kalispel Tribe of Indians, notes that the Kalispel people spaced their children carefully so as to not deplete the land. He estimates that the population stayed relatively steady at about three thousand people for thousands of years.[9]

The Kalispel people were joined on the shores of Lake Pend Oreille by the Coeur d'Alene, Kootenai, and Salish tribes. They shared the bounty of these waters with these neighbors, and in turn, the Kalispel were welcomed to fish, hunt, and gather on their neighbors' homelands. This sharing of resources and space brought communities together and led to family ties through marriage. As each new generation of babies grew, the webs of relationships between bands grew too.

It's hard not to imagine the bluff being an important landmark for the Kalispel people, as it marks the outlet of Lake Pend Oreille. Archaeological evidence suggests that winter encampments for the Kalispel people were often located along the river edges at the outlet of a creek. Several archaeological digs in the area, including Dover, have produced a variety of artifacts that make clear that this site was used by the Kalispel people.[10] In the summer, the bluff would have provided welcome shade as families canoed between fishing sites, following the spawning schedules of various fish species.

THE FIRST SETTLERS

North Idaho is remote, and, as a result, the Kalispel people avoided contact with white explorers and settlers longer than most other Indigenous people. The first white men to the region were led by David Thompson, a surveyor and explorer from the North West Company, who arrived in 1807. By 1809, Thompson had helped establish a trading post, the Kully-spel House, thirteen miles upstream from the bluff. His journals reveal that even before the post was built, tribes from across the region had arrived via the lakes and rivers, a vast system that connects the Indigenous people of the Columbia River Basin. Thompsons reports: "Sixteen canoes of Coeur d'Alenes . . . Fifteen 'strange Indians from the west,' who may have belonged to the San Poil and Okanagan tribes . . . Two 'Green Wood' [Nez Perce] men brought beaver, muskrat and bear pelts [to] exchange."[11]

Next to arrive were Jesuit priests, who traveled throughout the region starting in 1841. They marveled at the forests they found around Lake Pend Oreille, writing in their journals that the forest "is certainly a wonder of its kind; there is probably nothing similar to it in America." It was the size of the trees that stunned them:

> Really every tree which it contains is enormous in its kind. The birch, elm and beech, generally small elsewhere . . . swell out here to twice their size . . . cedars of four and five fathoms in circumference are here very common; we saw some six, and I measured one forty-two feet in circumference. A cedar of four fathoms, lying on the ground measured more than two hundred feet in length. The delicate branches of these noble trees, entwine themselves above the beech and elm; their fine, dense and evergreen foliage forming an arch through which the sun's rays never penetrate.[12]

Military expeditions looking for a mountain pass to cross the northern Rocky Mountains began in the 1850s and brought more contact between the Indigenous peoples and colonial settlers. Lieutenant Rufus Saxton, on one such expedition, describes the Kalispel as being "perfectly civil," and added that they "seemed to feel proud, rich, and independent."[13]

The arrival of priests and other early colonial settlements exposed the Kalispel people to diseases they had no protection against. By 1850 the diseases brought by colonial settlement had already reduced the number of Kalispel people to between six hundred and eight hundred people. When these military men wrote that the Kalispel people were proud and rich, their numbers had already been reduced by 75 percent in only fifty years.[14]

Lieutenant Saxton would also write upon seeing the lake for the first time in 1853 that "on the shores of the lake are many fine meadows, covered with luxuriant grass. The lake is navigable, and no doubt that in a coming time, not very remote, its repose will be broken by the shrill scream and the paddles of the steamboat. I met many Indians, fine specimens of the race."[15] This seeming sadness about the fate of this place was likely informed by Saxton's knowledge of what had happened in the United States beyond the shores of Lake Pend Oreille.

The predictions of change and the shrill scream of steam engines would come to pass in 1866, but it was not just steamboats that would transform the landscape. The twin forces of timber and the railroad would radically alter the Pend Oreille watershed and the lives of the Kalispel people. Those forces were imagined in 1869 when the Northern Pacific Railroad surveyed the area looking for a northern route for a transcontinental rail line. During that scouting trip, they noted that the shores of the lake would provide "a glorious field here for saw mills."[16] The surveyors saw a gentle grade across the Rocky Mountains, forests with trees to use for railroad ties, and plenty of water to move those trees from the forests to mills.

Of course, the surveyors and other colonial settlers completely misunderstood the relationships that sustained those forests. For thousands of years, the waterways of the Pend Oreille watershed were transportation routes that sustained vast communities of Kalispel people who thrived from the bounty around them. The Kalispel people had spent thousands of years in equilibrium with the wilderness and the waterways, managing their population and usage of the natural resources. When white surveyors arrived, they assumed that the thriving forests were natural and "virginal," compartmentalizing the health of the ecosystem from the practices of the communities that had subsisted off those spaces for hundreds of generations. By failing to understand that the lifeworld of this space was a result of a complex and reverent human relationship with it, these colonial settlers saw the West as a limitless place of extraction.

Most histories of North Idaho start with the arrival of the railroad and the mills. These histories might give a brief mention of David Thompson and the Kullyspel House, but they then move directly to the railroad's arrival. There is essentially no history of places like Dover and other small towns before their mills were established. This is a book about Dover, but of course, there was no "Dover" before settlers arrived. Instead, the communities that emerged at this time were a direct result of a Western, capitalist epistemology that sees the primary purpose of the natural world as a source of producing capital. The Kalispel people weathered floods and droughts; they expected the ebb and flow of the river. But that change is not equivalent to the kinds of change that exploded in 1881, when the first tree was cut along the shores of Lake Pend Oreille to make railroad ties. Those ties, soaked in creosote and lined up one after another for many hundreds of miles, completed the northern transcontinental railroad, linking Seattle, Washington, to St. Paul, Minnesota. This linked the shores of the Pacific Ocean to those of the East Coast and opened the riches of the Northern Rockies—the ore, timber, wheat, and beef—to the world.

The settlement of the American West is often romanticized as an era of democracy and opportunity, where diverse groups of Euro-American settlers could create new lives and new prosperity for themselves in a space freed from the social and economic structures of more developed spaces. But the settlement of the West was not open and free to all, and the primary beneficiaries of this process were not hearty settlers and their families but already-prosperous businessmen, who were essentially given millions of acres from the US government to expand their wealth.

Workers building the Northern Pacific came eastward from Spokane, Washington, into the panhandle of Idaho, crossed Lake Pend Oreille, and followed the gentle grade of the Clark Fork River into Montana. When the railroad arrived, the community of Sandpoint was little more than a bar and a hotel with just a few residents. It was immediately inundated with railroad workers. For two years, upwards of a thousand men, two-thirds of them Chinese, worked to build the tracks along the lake.[17]

A detailed report of a camp just upriver from Sandpoint found the site "held 2,600 Chinese and 1,400 Caucasians."[18] Housed in separate quarters, the Chinese workers, all men, kept their own stores, restaurants, and doctors. In communities all along the route of the Northern Pacific, including Sandpoint, Chinese men attempted to return after the railroad was completed to build lives along the rail line they had built. In some, Chinese settlers were quickly run out of town by white settlers. In one local newspaper report, locals expressed outrage that a Chinese-owned restaurant had the audacity to hire a white woman as a server. In an advertisement in that same paper, businesses made special note that the staff at their shops included no Chinese workers. The anti-Chinese sentiment also took more violent forms. In 1887 a group of thirty-four Chinese miners was massacred on the Snake River in Idaho. Several men were put on trial, but no one ever served time for the murders.[19]

Today, Bonner County is one of the whitest in the nation, at 96.5 percent white. Among locals, there is a common sentiment that this is somehow natural. This sentiment carefully reimagines the American West, ignoring the 8,000–10,000-year history of Indigenous people in North Idaho and the disproportionate work Chinese laborers did to create the scaffolding that allowed communities in the West to grow and flourish along the railroads built for them.

One of the most extreme changes that the railroad brought to the West was that it "provided transportation for land-hungry western settlers; making accessible natural resources and agricultural products abundant in western land."[20] The Northern Pacific cut a path to the heart of Lake Pend Oreille, and the company didn't simply want settlers to buy a ticket on the train. They wanted to sell them land. Decades before the final spike was driven in 1883, the Northern Pacific had lobbied the US government for subsidies to construct the line. They were given over forty million acres of land—a landmass roughly the size of the state of Wisconsin. For every mile of track built, the federal government handed over 12,800 acres—double that amount in the territories—to the company.[21]

As soon as the line was completed, the Northern Pacific began advertising to potential settlers in sort of guidebooks published by Rand McNally, telling them that the railroad has "about 2,000,000 acres of land in Northern Idaho" and extolling the beauty of Lake Pend Oreille. A sketch of the lake accompanies the text, encouraging settlers to move to North Idaho. In it, two presumably Kalispel people occupy the center of the image, paddling a sturgeon-nosed canoe across placid water. Behind them is a treed bluff framed by boulders bearing a remarkable resemblance to the bluff in Dover.[22] Ironically, the idyllic imagery of Native peoples was used to facilitate the often-violent displacement of those peoples from the land.

Throughout this process of settlement and land acquisitions, however, the Indigenous peoples of the area continued to live on the land, subsisting while their traditional lands became increasingly crowded by white settlement. In an interview, in fact, one longtime resident in Dover remembers sharing the land with the Kalispel people during his childhood in Dover in the 1920s. "They used to camp on just the other side of where we lived," he remembered. "They'd come in there in the summertime. They'd go up to Sandpoint, down to the city where the city beach is now and have a powwow there. I don't know how long the powwows lasted. I can barely remember it because I was probably only five, six years old. . . . Folks used to go—my brothers would go down there and trade them deerskins for moccasins." Powwows on the city beach would soon be unthinkable as more and more white settlers poured into North Idaho.

It was not simply settlers, however, who bought up the majority of the land that was taken from the Kalispel people. Instead, the Northern Pacific sold most of the land it was given by the US government to "just a handful of corporations," which would, in turn, harvest it for timber in North Idaho.[23] The empire of Frederick Weyerhaeuser, still a household name in some North Idaho communities, was built from these land sales. In 1894, Weyerhaeuser bought 900,000 acres of railroad land. "In all Weyerhaeuser purchased some 1.5 million acres of timberland from the Northern Pacific, roughly eighty percent of its total holdings . . . [making his company] the second-largest holder of timberlands in the United States, with holdings totaling roughly 95 billion board feet of standing merchantable timber."[24] In most places, Weyerhaeuser paid just six dollars an acre, and he shrewdly refused to pay that rate on land that was not timbered.[25]

The fate of Sandpoint, Idaho, is a case study of this history. Humbird Mill put Sandpoint on the map in the 1880s. It was built along the shore of Lake Pend Oreille and was partially owned by Weyerhaeuser. Most of the land used to supply the mill was either purchased from the Northern Pacific Railroad or bought directly from the federal or state government (Idaho became a state in 1890). Records from Humbird Mill show that, of the 159,000 acres acquired from 1901 to 1910, they paid an average of $5.60 an acre.[26] For comparison, you could buy two "Universal Wolf Tooth Forceps for extracting wolf teeth" or three ventilated false beards on a wire for $6.[27] In other words, unimaginably huge tracts of land were essentially given away to the already rich and connected. Weyerhaeuser was a close friend and neighbor of the railroad baron James J. Hill, also known as "the Empire Builder" of the Northwest.[28]

It was Hill who would put Dover on the map when he finished the second railroad that would skirt the shores of Lake Pend Oreille, the Great Northern. The Great Northern crossed the river downstream and ran along the edge of Dover. It opened up more timberland for logging.

LABOR CONDITIONS AND STRIFE

At the time, mill owners did not just own mills; they owned the land that they logged. They bought vast tracts of land, logged them, then processed those logs. It kept the men they hired busy year-round. During the winter, teams of men would live in the mountains, felling trees. The logs could then be hauled on sleighs across the snow and ice to the river or lake, where they could make their way to the mill to be processed during the warmer months.

As soon as these workers made their homes in mill towns like Dover, they and the corporations found themselves in tension, a tension that would continue to animate conflict in Dover over a hundred years later. Mill workers and other settlers in the region sought to create jobs and communities that would sustain their families. They were interested not simply in laboring but in asserting the dignity of their work while building communities that they hoped would last for generations. The owners of the land and the mills, by contrast, were most often simply concerned with extracting as much value as possible from their investments. Communities and families were only an unintentional by-product of that process.

This tension manifested at first around working conditions, which were terribly dangerous in lumber camps. Deaths were common, and the living conditions for the men were abysmal. In an interview, one old-time Dover resident shared stories about the dangers of the work: "My dad got blew up with dynamite when he was twenty-one years old. He was blasting stumps for a road ramp by Bonners for the county. He set a charge underneath the stump. Him and his brother . . . they got outta the way, and for a long time, and nothin' happened. My dad went up to dig it out, and he's diggin' the charger out when it went off." These kinds of stories were common as men worked six days a week, ten hours a day.

The dining hall was a bright spot for most timber camps but betrayed the demands of the job. The US Department of Agriculture (USDA) recommended that men consume eight thousand calories a day to keep up their work. A recommended breakfast, for example, included all of the following: oatmeal mush, doughnuts, rye bread, cornbread and syrup, cornmeal cookies (made with corn syrup), apple butter, creamed potatoes, coffee, and codfish cakes. After "supper," the men could look forward to retiring to a bunkhouse filled with wooden bed frames. The men had to bring their own straw to fill the beds and sheets to make them. The beds were often ridden with lice, as the camps typically had no running water, thus nowhere for the men to wash themselves or their clothing. Years later, timber workers would still remember the stench of a bunkhouse filled with men removing their wet socks, unwashed for an entire season, to dry by the fire.[29]

The summers offered slightly better conditions, because the men could come back to town, often rejoining their families. But the work was dangerous. Imagine huge logs that had to be moved down the lake using little more than the flow of water and hooked poles. In addition, mills were prone to fire, but, because the working conditions were so bad, it was often difficult for mill owners to distinguish between naturally caused fires and those caused by industrial sabotage at the hands of disgruntled workers.

Workers did not just push back against these conditions by burning mills. Starting at the turn of century, North Idaho became a hotbed for labor organizing. The conditions for radical organizing were ideal because the jobs themselves—millwork and mining—brought workers together and there was a clear vertical structure between the workers, managers, and owners.

The first mill in Dover, which was originally, though briefly, named "Welty," opened in 1907, and conditions were no better there. Mill workers lived in tents and tar paper shacks. From 1907 to 1922, the newspaper focused on the equipment at the mill more than the people. We learn, for example, that "this mill is equipped with a 9-foot Allis & Chalmers 14-inch double-cut band saw and one Mershon 6-foot horizontal band re-saw" and that "the mill has a capacity of 90,000 feet in 10 hours and employs 100 people."[30]

But the Dover mill continued to find its place in North Idaho history thanks to the radical labor organizing that emerged from the mines and forests of the region. Miner strikes to the south resulted in Idaho's Silver Valley being "placed under martial law twice."[31] The radical Industrial Workers of the World, or the "Wobblies," worked to organize all the workers in the region into a single union allied against the capitalist class. Their work in North Idaho focused on the fight for an eight-hour workday. When timber workers in North Idaho weren't successful in their demands after a long strike in the summer of 1918, they used industrial sabotage as part of their "strike at work" strategy, whereby equipment and timber were destroyed, or the men simply quit working after eight hours. Workers in Dover became involved with the Wobblies, and unsalable "short logs were found at the Dover Mill in increasing numbers during 1917, 1918, and 1919."[32] Despite twenty workers standing trial for their involvement with the Wobblies, lumber workers did win an eight-hour workday, a forty-eight-hour workweek, and time-and-a-half overtime pay. They also won better conditions at both mills and logging camps: steel bunks, clean bedding, electric lights, showers, and laundry.[33]

In retaliation, the lumber bosses immediately began contracting out timber collection to avoid meeting the demands for better housing, as workers fought for and won additional benefits in the lumber mills and mines of North Idaho (and across the United States). As one boss pointed out, "hours don't count when men work for themselves."[34] Men were paid piecemeal for the timber they cut. Managers also began decreasing the number of people required in the mills by increasing the mechanization of labor. Trucks and bulldozers began to replace men, horses, and sleighs. These dynamics continue even today.

For most of the people of Dover, the history of their community is not born with the first mill but rather with the arrival of A. C. White, who purchased the mill in 1922. White had run a successful mill eleven miles downriver, in Laclede, Idaho. Like others, he had taken advantage of the new Great Northern, which was built along the north side of the river, and the Spokane International (SI), built in 1906. White purchased a mill along both routes and the timberland to supply it. This helps explain how "one-third of the timberlands in the Inland Northwest changed owner-ship" from 1900 to 1910.[35]

On August 18, 1922, the history of Dover was forged when White's mill in Laclede erupted in a terrible fire, burning an estimated $700,000 worth of timber and equipment. White decided that he had cleared the most accessible timber around that mill, so he used his insurance payout from the fire to float what was left of the mill (including homes and other buildings that survived) up the river to start over in Dover.

Dover exists, then, because a rail line was laid, and because enormous tracts of the American West were wrenched away from Indigenous people and given to the railroad, which turned around and sold them to already rich men to increase their fortunes, built on the backs of men who often worked in desperate conditions. Like many records from the time, those documenting what the mill land sold for are lost to history, likely destroyed by later fires, but if A. C. White paid the $6 an acre that most land was going for, it would have cost $1,800 for the three hundred acres of land that made up the mill site along the shores of the Pend Oreille, less than a modest, mail-order house from the Sears, Roebuck and Co. catalog. In a little more than a hundred years, the newest owner would take out a $15,000,000 loan for the property and its improvements.

From 1922 to 1928, when a fire burned the mill down, White's workers in Dover continued producing thousands of feet of lumber a day. This was slowed down only by a warm winter in 1926 that made it difficult to get timber out of the forest and to the mill. When it was closed by fire, fol-lowed shortly by White's death in 1928, it was estimated that the com-pany still had "50 million feet of timber to cut and has options on millions more." In addition, the newspaper notes, "there is plenty of timber avail-able for a long time run of the mill."[36]

Even with the mill closed, settlers continued arriving in Dover for the promise of the great American West. A second group of old-timer residents arrived amid the Great Depression, displaced from the Great Plains as a result of the Dust Bowl. One resident who had arrived in Dover during this period remembers that "there wasn't hardly any people lived in Dover. I think there were only ten families lived here in the '30s before the Dust Bowlers started moving in." They settled in Dover because, after the 1928 fire and the economic downturn had closed the mill, the houses were empty and cheap. Another longtime resident similarly remembers arriving in a wagon with her family fleeing the Dust Bowl: "We moved in one week. The Wallsons moved in the next week, and the Reynolds moved in the next week, here, and across the way, the Andersons. . . . The middle house, Frahms did live in it, when we moved here. The end was this Dover store. It was run by a lady. We picked the middle house because there was a school here."

For the Kalispel people, however, the logging and settlement of the region nearly spelled their complete demise. By 1914, little more than a hundred years after their first contact with white people, there were only 114 Kalispel people. In only a few generations, the number of Kalispel—grandmas and grandpas, aunts and uncles, mothers and fathers, sons and daughters—was reduced by 96 percent.[37] This small group of survivors would face generations of grief as they were forced from their homeland. They did not just lose nearly everyone they held dear, they lost their homeland as dams were built that flooded meadows and beaches and radically altered the habitat of the fish they relied upon. And when the Kalispel people continued, despite these losses, to hunt and gather traditional foods, laws were passed that attempted to take that from them as well. The Kalispel people's tragedy, then, is like that of nearly every other Indigenous group in North America. In an interview with a local reporter, Francis Cullooyah wondered "how his ancestors survived such dramatic losses. 'I would not be able to live very well. I wouldn't be able to go through it.'"[38]

BOOMS AND BUSTS

The timber economy has always been beset by boom-and-bust cycles that most directly impact working people. The "Turner thesis," or "Frontier thesis," posits that the period of US colonial expansion before 1890 marked a period during which white immigrants and settlers experienced true democracy and freedom, but that period came to an abrupt end in the 1890s with the arrival of timber, mining, and railroad barons to the American West. While critiqued for failing to consider the impact and role that the genocide of Indigenous people had in this process, Turner's analysis does effectively articulate the profound changes that characterize this period. He argues that these barons used the West as a sort of colony for the East—extracting material resources from the West back to the East. It must be noted that they did this only through the exploitation of the labor of American, European, and Chinese workers.

But throughout this period of exploitation, towns like Dover bound themselves together to form thriving communities, often despite their treatment at the hands of the capitalist class. Amid the mill in Dover opening and closing, being bought and sold, residents persevered in creating a life for themselves, in creating a tightly woven community. Neighbor kids married, and Dover tangled together into a web of friends and family who watched out for each other. They met at the sandy beach to teach their kids to swim and threw decades of summer picnics.

For many Dover old-timers, the origin story of their homes, church, and community center being floated upriver, arriving by boat and coming to rest in Dover, is their origin story too, since these places are central to their histories. Today, the walls of the community hall display well-known photos of buildings being floated up the river. People tell stories about the float being so smooth that families left their furniture in place for the trip upstream. Some of the residents were born in Dover to parents who came for work in the mill or the railroad, or to farm, or build houses, or paint newly built houses, or teach the children who lived in them.

A. C. White remains a sort of legendary figure in Dover, and most residents still speak of him in revered terms. He was said to be unusually kind and generous. Even today, residents remain grateful that he converted his summer home into their church and floated the homes they still occupy up the river, making a sort of outpost into a full-fledged community.

As revered as A. C. White is in Dover, however, it is the people of Dover who made it a community, not the mill owner. The town's admiration for

1.1. The community hall (*right*) and church (*left*) were both floated upriver when the mill in Laclede burned down in the 1920s. They have served Dover families for nearly one hundred years.

White reflects a popular narrative in US culture in which business owners, by providing jobs, are credited with creating the thriving communities sustained by those jobs. But communities like Dover that dotted the American West in this period were simply by-products of capitalist expansion. The railroads were not meant to connect these communities to the world. Instead, they were built in order to move and combine human labor and the abundance of natural resources in the region. The timber mills were not built to support these small towns but to deliver timber to markets. The towns that sprang up were an afterthought, populated by far-flung settlers, and were not intended to last after the timber was finally cleared. But the people of Dover (and communities like it) settled in for the long haul, building ties of friendship and camaraderie that would sustain them for generations, tying them to the space in ways that mill owners like White probably could not have imagined.

Communities are organized around the visions of the people who build them, and the people who built North Idaho, lumber barons like Weyerhaeuser, did not create it with a long-term vision in place. They saw timber extraction as a one-time activity. A 1901 editorial in the *Kootenai County Republican* lays this out clearly: "We do not expect our timber resources to last forever, but just long enough to give us a start in other directions."[39] In other words, a timber economy was never intended to support families in North Idaho—and it has only done so occasionally.

That said, A. C. White did lay the groundwork for Dover's close-knit community by embracing the power of communal spaces. White, a deeply religious man whose brother was the preacher at the church, was said to have given the people of Dover perpetual access to the old beach as long as the church was operational (although documentation of this gift is lacking, a sticking point in later debates about the development). This was to ensure that they would have a place to perform baptisms.

Dover thrived, then, because many of the spaces around it, like the beach, were considered shared common land. Old-timer residents remembered everyone keeping a milk cow. The cows were turned out in the morning to graze in the fields around the mill and railroad tracks, and they came home in the evening to be milked, providing the families with much-needed food. Gene Nelson remembers, "If people wanted to keep the cows out, they built a fence. It wasn't the other way around. You didn't have to build a fence to keep them in." Of course, that this land could essentially supplement his workers' income by providing food, and that the beach might encourage people to stay in this place to enjoy its beauty, may have certainly been part of White's calculus.

In the years after World War II, this sense of community pride and collective labor would be supplemented by the booming of the timber industry. Like many places, the best years for working people in North Idaho were in the boom years after that war.

After the mill changed hands several times, it came to be owned by the Brown family in 1941, who called it the Pack River Lumber Company. In 1944, Brown negotiated with the Northern Pacific Railroad for one of the "largest timber and land transfers ever made" in this part of the country.[40] With a huge amount of cheap timberland at its disposal and a booming economy, Pack River retooled the old mill in 1955 to produce a product for the future: "decorative wall board." A headline exclaimed, "Interior Designers Enthusiastic about Board."[41] This enthusiasm led homeowners and builders from coast to coast to cover walls with wood paneling.

Brown's changes in Dover perfectly align with broader changes during this period. The postwar years were a boon to the timber industry, because the demand for new housing expanded the demand for lumber, spurred by a host of government programs, such as new homes built for returning GIs, funded by the GI Bill. Government funding for new highway programs also allowed for the creation of suburbs. In addition, government investment in new technologies, often originally for the military, created new products for old mills to deliver. The industry grew into "a true 'wood products' enterprise," where "products like particleboard, pulp paper, and formaldehyde were gathered from lumber wastes formerly discarded" and turned into materials to bring to market.[42]

The industry also benefited from technological changes in machinery for the wood: "heavy trucks and portable power saws" and technological advancements in the mills allowed timber to be processed more efficiently.[43] For Brown, these changes meant buying land that had once been too far removed from the railroads and the mill to be harvested.

If working families survived the often-volatile decades between 1900 and 1945 by filling in their unmet needs with the riches of the land—hunting, fishing, firewood, and communal land for milk and egg production—they survived from 1945 to 1985 because of a booming economy that was structured, briefly after World War II, to share the riches of that economy with the white working class through high wages, good benefits, and low-priced goods.

In this period, young men from Dover, whose parents never dreamed that they would enter college, graduated with advanced degrees. And those families who stayed used their wages to build modest homes in the community or remodel old mill houses. They filled their yards with cheerful flowerbeds, while trips the grocery store replaced milking cows.

CONCLUSION

The people of Dover still fished and swam in the waters around the bluff as the decades after WWII wore on, but the energy crisis in the mid-1970s marked the beginning of the end of this boom, and the ability of a high school graduate to support a family on a forty-hour-a-week job slowly became more and more impossible.

This postwar period of economic stability would alter the town of Dover's expectations as a community, as it would for many white working-class communities. Working families are consistently told to look to these best years for what is "typical," when, in fact, those years were the result of a set of very particular and unusual economic and social arrangements. This is especially true in the American West, which was built around a few industries that are deeply linked to the health of the broader national and global economies: the timber market is a near-perfect reflection of the housing market, for example. Because of this relationship, the short history of the American West is the history of boom-and-bust cycles, because our economies have so few buffers. The long boom period for timber after WWII would bring unprecedented levels of prosperity to towns like Dover, but it was not meant to last.

As discussed in more detail in the next chapter, a tremendous amount of lumber is still produced in North Idaho each year, but the profits from that production flow into the pockets of far fewer families in the community because of the mechanization and consolidation of mills. The mill in Dover was eventually shuttered in 1989. As the timber and mining economies that had sustained the region struggled in the 1980s, the state accepted the blame for this and elected politicians who would usher in "right to work" laws in 1985 that marked the beginning of the end of Idaho's years of strong labor organizing.

The decline in timber jobs in the region, then, was just the next phase in the tensions between workers and owners. Those with capital and power sought to maximize their profits at the expense of the workers and communities that had gleaned a modicum of prosperity in the industry's boom years after WWII. But for communities like Dover, those years had raised their expectations around their labor and the community, fostering a sense of communal pride that they would cling to as their town faced a seemingly endless series of challenges in the 1980s and 1990s.

2

Water, Water Everywhere

WORK AT THE mill in Dover continued to be somewhat precarious for decades after WWII. However, the broad labor gains won by the workers around the region in both logging and mining meant that people in the area could almost always find a job that provided a good wage and benefits. Through the early 1980s, workers in Dover were consistently able to piece together employment at the Dover mill, at other mills in the area, or even in mining camps in order to provide a steady income for their families.

Dover resident Sharon Miller, a woman who had arrived there as a Dust Bowl refugee via covered wagon, remembered her husband getting laid off from the Dover mill every year in the 1940s, but he was always able to find work. She noted:

> They would lay you off every winter, about every December. I said they kill Santy Claus every year. [My husband] would go to work someplace [else] . . . I think he worked three or four times up at the mines. You know, he didn't mind that either. That's amazing to me, 'cuz you're underground. He didn't mind that. He went all dressed up to work, and then you took your shower and stuff, and put on your good clothes again, took off your mining clothes and hung 'em up to dry. They had a wonderful

2.1. An undated but likely midcentury photo of the mill in Dover. The bluff sits in the upper-right-hand corner with the old Dover beach directly to the left of the bluff. Original mill homes, the community hall, and the community church are in the upper-left-hand corner. Photo courtesy of the Bonner County Historical Society and Museum.

room-and-board place at Kellogg. They fed 'em and everything. They took that out of their wages. Before they even got their check, they took their room and board out of their wages, which was okay, too. He had money to send home, to bring home.

Miller's husband's work was dirty and dangerous, but it was part of a web of opportunity that led to economic stability for families. This opportunity lasted for decades. There was always somewhere for men to find a job with decent pay somewhere in North Idaho.

These opportunities were certainly in place after WWII, when the demand for lumber to build housing for returning GIs meant that the mill in Dover reopened and (mostly) stayed open. But even if the mill in Dover had not always provided stable employment, it had been one of many mills in which to find work. And when mill work was not available, one could head south about ninety miles to work in the mines of the Silver Valley, where men could live for part of the year while sending money back to their families (as Sharon's late husband had done).

The mining and timber industries needed workers, and this created an economic structure that allowed communities to thrive, especially as timber and mining were interlinked with the railroad. All of the long-time residents of Dover recalled that they and their parents had worked at a job that was at least tangentially supported by these industries. They worked for the railroad, or as farmers, house painters, or teachers, or "worked in the woods," providing the timber necessary to keep the mills running. From about 1948 through the early 1980s, "a guy could show up with a pair of work gloves and get a job," a former worker recalled.

As a result, most families in Dover in this period often resembled the idealized vision of a working-class American family: the father headed off in the morning to physical labor while mothers busied themselves with housework and the children were left to run and play in wild spaces. Weekends meant dads coaching the River Rats baseball team on the baseball diamond—built down the road from the mill—and families picnicking at the beach. Most of the people who remain in old Dover today are folks whose entire families grew up together there in this period, building a life around the mill and the beach. They recalled, with deep fondness, raising their children in Dover.

But things were about to change. Communities such as Dover had come to rely on the financial stability provided by the prosperity of timber, mining, and the railroads. When the economic structures underpinning this prosperity shifted, however, the employment opportunities upon which so many families had depended dried up, and the town of Dover was left to deteriorate—literally—as the town's infrastructure, which had been tied up with the mill, crumbled all around them.

Towns like Dover felt the sting of these changes, both economically and culturally. The relative stability and prosperity of the postwar period led people in rural communities such as Dover to think that they mattered, that their prosperity was important to corporations in the region, and to the culture as a whole. They were the workers whose timber built homes for families all around the country. They did the dirty jobs upon which the national economy was based. They imagined that they not only worked *for* corporations that owned mills and mines and rail lines but also *with* those businesses to build strong, wholesome communities in the wild spaces of the American West. The postwar economic boom reinforced this narrative, leading the people of Dover (and so many other towns like it) to believe that they enjoyed relative stability based on mutual respect between them and their employers.

As the mill's operations dwindled starting in the 1980s, however, the residents of Dover learned just how little their town mattered when the timber industry changed. Workers and mill towns in the Pacific Northwest became more and more obsolete in the face of mechanization and globalization, even though most people would blame environmentalists and the federal government. In the wake of these changes, the people of Dover learned that their town's prosperity was not a priority of the mill owners or other corporations in the region—a stable, family-friendly community was simply a side effect of the postwar boom. A healthy community didn't matter to anyone except the families in Dover.

Residents of Dover learned this lesson quickly as their water system fell into disrepair during the timber crisis of the 1980s. Faced with shifting economic conditions, a succession of mill owners neglected the town's aging water system, which had historically been managed by the mill, leaving the citizens of Dover to struggle for years with water shortages, boil orders, and ancient pipes. As the community's infrastructure was left to rot, the people of Dover worked tirelessly to remedy their water woes. Of course, once the town scrambled to build a new water system (with grants, loans for low-income towns, and higher taxes on their already strained incomes), the owners of the mill now suddenly stood to profit immensely, as they owned a prime parcel of waterfront property, complete with a brand-new water system.

Dover's "water woes" were not an accident. The community's water system was left to crumble by the same people who got rich there, illustrating the fragility of communities built to support multinational projects of capitalism. The citizens of Dover may have helped to create wealth for the various timber companies that owned the mills, but when their labor became less and less necessary, it also became increasingly clear that the needs of the community simply did not matter to the mill owners. In fact, the destruction of their community (often literally, in the form of crumbling infrastructure) was part of a deliberate process of devaluation that explicitly benefited the corporate landowners who had operated the mill. The decay of the community's water system, while devastating to the residents, created an opportunity for economic gain for the mill's owners and later the developers of the mill site. By allowing the water system to decay to the point at which it was no longer usable, the owners of the mill property could leverage Dover's literal need for water to their advantage by pushing the community to rezone it.

The leveraging of Dover's water woes was part of a much larger project in this period in which industries that were no longer profitable were left to decay when they failed to generate substantial profits. This happened most often at the expense of the people whose labor created the opportunities for corporate profit in the first place and who were bound through familial and cultural ties to a place. This decay served the purpose of keeping the cost of the property low until it could be reimagined under a different vision for investment and development. Scholars describe how this process leads to gentrification by increasing "the rent gap," that is, the process of devaluation and subsequent reinvestment that creates "the disparity between the potential ground rent level and the actual ground rent capitalized under the present land use."[1] Neil Smith saw this rent gap as central to the process of urban gentrification, and other scholars, including Eliza Darling[2] and Peter Nelson and J. Dwight Hines,[3] noted that it is similarly essential to rural gentrification. Allowing for the decay or destruction of communities, then, allows landowners to drive down the price of land while also keeping the people who might want to own it, including municipalities, too poor to afford it. Landowners and developers can then reimagine the space, often through zoning but more often simply through design, so that those with wealth to invest can once again reap profit off the same land.

CHANGES IN THE TIMBER INDUSTRY

At the height of Idaho's lumber-producing days after WWII, 311 mills were operating. By 1990, that number was reduced to 80. Only 27 were operating by 2011.[4] A 2001 article in the *Washington Times* reported that "Idaho and the rest of the Pacific Northwest have watched the timber economy plummet over the last decade, taking with it a dozen mills and at least 30,000 jobs."[5] The mill in Dover was one of these casualties. It was shuttered in 1989, only months after workers at the mill voted to unionize. Those workers would be the last ones to work at the mill in Dover.

As mill jobs declined, so did the benefits and stability that went along with them. Amy Brown remembers raising her children in Dover in the 1970s while her husband (now ex) worked at the mill. "It was a union job," she said. "They had really good benefits. [The health insurance for] all of my kids was almost totally paid for. We didn't have to pay on them as we went along, or after they were born, or whatever. The little bit we had to pay, it was easy after the insurance took care of most of it. They made good wages. They had overtime, paid really well for overtime."

That all changed in the mid-1980s. Tim Casten remembers this period "when the lumber industry started hitting hard times . . . it was just a sad time, because that was where a lot of people worked and it hurt the economy when it closed." But it wasn't just the jobs that the community lost when the mill closed in 1989. Casten added that they also lost "the old taste of Dover, where it was a close-knit community where people knew each other and talked to each other and it was just a friendly town. People knew each other and said hello to each other and met once in a while and congregated in the old community hall and those kinds of things."

Ironically, for many places, the 1980s was a time of economic gain, but for working-class people in extractive industries, particularly in the rural West, this period marked a dramatic downturn. As Kenneth Deavers noted, "the combined pressures during the 1980s of a long-term structural decline in natural resource–based industries (especially in agricultural employment) and a newly emerging industrial restructuring of the nonfarm economy (the result of an increasing integration of the US and world economies) left rural areas at a competitive disadvantage."[6]

Perhaps the most significant and often least discussed cause of this downturn was automation and consolidation. While the number of mills that closed between 1979 and 2006 is striking—reducing the total from 133 to 38 (and another 11 would close by 2011)—the amount of lumber produced in North Idaho actually increased in nearly every reported period between 1979 and 2006, from 930,446 thousand board feet in 1979 to 1,213,987 in 2006.[7]

These seeming contradictions are explained by the closure of small mills and the growth of much larger ones that simply needed fewer people to do the same work because of the rapid mechanization of the industry. Repeating what happened sixty years earlier, when workers demanded fair compensation for their labor, the industry responded with rapid technological interventions to replace humans with machines. One researcher noted that "nationwide during the 1980s production in lumber mills rose by almost 2%/year and employment at those mills declined by 2%/year," while "labor demand in the pulp and paper industry [producing timber by-products] was also falling as a result of technological change, with labor productivity increasing at 3.1%/year between 1975 and 1996."[8] Thus, precisely in the period when workers in the timber industries were becoming more prosperous, jobs disappeared as people were replaced by machines.

And it wasn't just the timber industry that shed laborers while becoming more productive. The other important extractive industry in North Idaho, mining, was also undergoing rapid technological innovations that made workers obsolete while continuing to produce record amounts of ore.

These changes were dire for Dover, because it meant that not only was the entire region undergoing rapid economic changes but that when the mill in Dover closed, mills around the region were also closing. And the old standby of going to work in the mines was also no longer an option. Clarence Hill describes the way even the parking lots changed in Dover: "When I first came here, you'd drive to town, and the town would be full of pickup trucks because they're all working at the mill, at the Dover mill. Now you don't see so many pickup trucks. You see cars."

For the people who relied on the timber industry for work, most of the blame for job losses fell on the federal government, thanks to new federal standards to protect fish and wildlife. The listing of the northern spotted

owl under the Endangered Species Act (1990) and federal wilderness protections—in particular, the Roadless Wilderness Act—took much of the
blame. While it is absolutely true that the supply of timber from federal
lands was dramatically limited by policies such as the Roadless Wilderness Act, some of the loss of timber from federal land was made up for by
increased logging on private lands and state lands.[9]

Of course, while there is little doubt that these policies substantially
reduced access to federal timberlands, researchers suggest that they actually resulted in less than 5 percent of the job losses experienced in the timber industry.[10] The expansion of automation happened at the same time
that the environmental movement gained a foothold in Northwest politics, meaning that federal environmental policies were held accountable
for job losses despite no evidence that less lumber was being produced in
North Idaho. In the press, the northern spotted owl, in particular, took a
great deal of blame for destroying the timber industry—even though it
isn't even found in Idaho. Unions also took the blame, and it's no surprise
that Idaho became a "right to work" state in 1985. It was the only state to
do so during the entire decade.

Moreover, timber and mining communities were understandably desperate to save the jobs they relied upon, and so unions and environmentalists became easy targets, despite data showing that mills in North
Idaho continued to pump out a huge amount of lumber while thousands
of people, mostly men, looked for jobs.

The shifting economic conditions caused by globalization also played
a major role in the decline of timber jobs in the Pacific Northwest. After
the passage of the North American Free Trade Agreement (NAFTA) in
1994, timber began pouring across the Canadian border to be processed
in North Idaho. By 1995, the tiny Eastport-Kingsgate border crossing was
the "sixth most trafficked along the western US-Canada border." According to Zach Hagadone, "90 percent of the trucks moving south were full
and 33 percent of those heading north were empty," meaning that Cana-
dians were logging the timber—clearly impacting logging jobs in Idaho—
but the logs were being processed in Idaho.[11]

This shift wasn't because of environmental regulations. It was far
simpler: the timber industry in Canada is subsidized, and it was cheaper
to buy Canadian timber. Certainly, federal policy dramatically changed

the timber industry, but those changes must be understood within a broader context, one that includes both the national and global pressure on the industry. Shawn Keough, one of North Idaho's Republican state senators, remembered "President Bill Clinton talking on the TV about how NAFTA was good for most of the USA 'except for small pockets here and there' and thinking that our little area of Idaho was dead center in one of those 'small pockets.'"[12] Writing for the Economic Policy Institute, Jeff Faux described the trade agreement as a "doctrine of socialism for capital and free markets for labor" that was used to "strengthen the ability of US employers to force workers to accept lower wages and benefits."[13]

Another often-overlooked factor in the decline of timber jobs in the Pacific Northwest is that companies like Weyerhaeuser moved their operations to the southern states and abroad. By the mid-1980s, with much of the easily accessed old-growth timber harvested in the Pacific Northwest, even before the Roadless Wilderness Act was in place, it became prohibitively expensive to build roads deep into the mountains. In the southern United States, softwood grows faster, the mountains are shorter, and wildfire poses less of a threat to huge swaths of timber. In short, logging timber in the Northwest was just getting more expensive.[14]

As this suggests, while federal policy became an easy scapegoat for the woes of timber workers in the Pacific Northwest, the constantly shifting practices of capitalism caused the decline in the industry. After all, almost all of the federal policies that locals blamed for job losses were put into practice *after* the mill in Dover closed in 1989. The reality was that the timber industry changed, and the decades of stability and prosperity that towns like Dover had built were now over.

In essence, this meant that the people who had worked the mills could no longer sell their labor to the mills in exchange for a wage. In a few short years, the value of their labor had radically decreased. At the same, the land the mill sat on, while relatively worthless as a mill, became extremely valuable when reimagined as a site for recreation-centered residences. This is a clear example of how the rent gap drives gentrification as the disparity between the potential, future value of the land is set in contrast to its current use. It is also a clear example of how the logic of capitalism centers wealth on private property rather than the value of the labor that creates that wealth. The people in Dover had labor to sell, which had been increasingly devalued due to automation; the mill owners had land to sell, which became more valuable explicitly because the timber economy was automated.

WATER WOES

The first inklings of the changes that would devastate many working-class families in the region came in the spring of 1973, when residents of Dover received letters from a law firm informing them that the Pack River Company, the current owners of the mill in Dover and, short of walking to the lake with a bucket, the town's only source of water, would "cease from supplying water to non-company owned properties."[15] In five short paragraphs, the mill explained to residents that while the mill had supplied the community with water since 1921,[16] on June 1, 1974, the Pack River would, "discontinue serving water to the private owners."[17] This was the same company that had upgraded the water tank only twenty-five years earlier to one designed to "meet requirements for Idaho state department of health" in order to supply the town of Dover and the mill with water.[18]

Knowing the loss of water would devastate the community, residents pushed back against the threat by Pack River. Marty Jones, Dover's long-time mayor, said that the community knew the law: "If you provide water for anybody, an entity or a neighbor or anything else, then legally you're required to keep providing that forever. There's no way you can just get out of it." Residents, then, became extra diligent in making sure their $1.50 a year water payments were recorded by the company. But they also prepared for the worst, unsure who, if anyone, could ultimately compel Pack River to continue providing water.

Sam Lenn also recalled making sure the water bill was paid and mentioned how residents worked to keep Pack River providing water. Lenn said, "Yeah, if they didn't pay, it'd then be privately owned. It wouldn't be considered part of the city. They would want you not to pay, but of course, Sandy [his wife] would pay ahead, and Patty [a friend and neighbor] would pay ahead . . . As long as anybody paid water bills, then they were bound to do it." Pack River appears to have conceded the issue. Residents continued diligently paying their bills, and the company continued providing water to the community but made no effort to maintain, let alone repair, the water system.

The town's water woes would only get worse as the timber industry declined, leading to decades of strife between the town and the owners of the mill and its associated property. The dwindling fortunes of the timber industry in the Pacific Northwest would lead the Pack River Company to sell the mill and property to Shamrock Investment Company in 1984. After buying the property, the investment company continued operating the mill for five years and continued providing water, as residents argued was their legal responsibility. The company, however, made some immediate changes.

First, they raised water rates from $1.50 a year—where they had remained for at least thirty years—to $18.00 a year.[19] Residents continued to diligently pay their bills, for fear that any lapse in payment would create a legal right for the investment company to quit providing water. Thirty years later, Amy Brown could still pull out a notice for payment on which a note had been neatly typed in the corner: "sent letter 4 Apr 1984 advising them of my payment and sent along a photocopy of the 1984 water check that had been returned to me canceled."[20] Residents believed that prompt payment was the difference between water and no water, and ultimately the difference between having a community and having no community.

Shortly after purchasing the property, Shamrock sent a letter to residents about their billing increase. The letter included a line that, particularly in retrospect, reads as ominous: "We have no plans for any change and will continue to keep the water system running *as best we can in its present condition*" (emphasis added).[21] That "present condition" was a water system that had been described as "ancient" in 1950.[22] A *Sandpoint News Bulletin* from that year enthusiastically describes the new 42,000-gallon steel tank that would replace the old wooden tank in Dover. The rest of the 1921 water system, however, was not upgraded. So when Shamrock said that the system would continue "in its present condition," they meant a water tank replaced in 1951 and the original 1920s infrastructure. The pipes that Shamrock inherited from Pack River, the pipes they never planned to upgrade, were wooden.

Dover resident Gene McPherson described these pipes as having been, "fixed, repaired, run over, broken, dug up many times over the years." By the 1980s, the water tank leaked so severely that there was "a regular creek flowing from it," and the system provided so little water pressure that "in many parts of town, so many people [couldn't] even flush their toilets."[23] An engineering firm that residents brought in to examine the system concluded that "essentially they have no water system."[24] So when Shamrock said it would continue to keep the water system running as best it could, it was referring to a condition so deteriorated that the newspaper described it as "something more at home in a Third World country than North Idaho."[25]

It was perhaps no surprise, then, that in August 1986 the Panhandle Health District found coliform bacteria in Dover's water supply and issued a boil order. Residents had no way of knowing that this boil order would remain in place for six long years. Children who grew up with it, like Sarah Walker, explained that her parents told her "there were bugs in the water that would make you sick and have diarrhea or whatever, and so we would have to boil water. It just became commonplace, because that's what we always did. To brush your teeth, you got water from the little cup out of the thing on the stove and brushed your teeth." Sarah, not even a kindergartner when the order went into effect, would be in fifth grade by the time it was lifted.

For Lorraine Johnson, the boil order came at the same time as her newborn daughter. She recalled the challenge of having a newborn baby and contaminated water: "When our daughter was born, the water was not potable. You had to boil the water. We have a brand-new baby in the house, and you can't even rinse out a baby bottle from the faucet. You have to boil it." She then added, laughing at the understatement, "It was somewhat difficult."

The challenges of the boil order were compounded by a barely functioning water pump that died anytime the power went off, a common problem, particularly from October to March, when power lines fell victim to tree limbs breaking under the weight of heavy snow. When the water pump died, the pump house would immediately begin flooding, sometimes with up to seven feet of water. Recalling the challenges those years presented, Evan Johnson shook his head and said, "The joke was that Dover needs water—flush your toilets."

In a newspaper interview during one outage, Patty Worth explained, "Every time the power flickers, it shuts off the pump. You have to get out there right away and turn it back on. If you don't get out there soon enough, it floods and you have to reprime it." Worth described repriming the pump as a "'quite involved process,' especially since the pump had no auxiliary power. That part of the system [hadn't] worked for quite a while."[26] This meant that Dover often went days without water while Shamrock Investment looked for someone to send out to fix it.

Residents quickly realized they were largely on their own to solve their water woes, and despite being surrounded by water in nearly every direction, the situation was dire. They responded by attempting to tackle short-term and long-term solutions. In the short term, they desperately tried to keep the water running. In a *Spokesman-Review* article, James Walker, the father of the woman who was not yet in kindergarten when the boil order was put in place, is pictured standing at the bottom of the pump house, tool in hand, looking exhausted after spending yet another freezing day working on the pump, something he not only did without compensation but for which he had to take time off work. "'I'm not a mechanic,' he said, throwing his hands up in the air." Emphasizing the point that he was indeed not a mechanic, the reporter noted, "Walker works with developmentally disabled adults." The frustration was compounded by the frequency of the outages that came without warning and often lasted for days. The *Spokesman-Review* article highlights this uncertainty and frustration, noting that "with the help of a few other volunteers, [Walker] managed to get the pump started Tuesday night only to have it die again Wednesday morning. He spent another day drying out equipment and by noon water was flowing from the taps again. 'For how long I don't know,' Walker said."[27]

The long-term solution was a new water system, but that too would prove slow and exhausting work. The first issue was that the town of Dover was not actually a town. The community of eighty households was an unincorporated city, meaning that they could not apply for most community grants and loans needed to subsidize the cost of a new water system. In spring of 1987, less than six months after the boil order was put in place, residents in the newly formed "Dover Water Association" asked the Bonner County commissioners to serve as sponsors for a Community Development Block Grant that would cover $350,000 of the estimated $700,000 cost of the new system. The commissioners agreed, and the application was submitted at the request of the citizen's committee in Dover.[28] The grant was not funded, in part because the Department of Commerce (DOC), which oversees the Community Development Block Grant program, did not believe that Dover had the rest of the funds necessary to complete the water system. Of course, the community couldn't apply for the other loans because it was not an incorporated city.

So in 1988, Dover incorporated. A prescient *Bonner County Daily Bee* article noted, "Historians will view Dover's 1988 incorporation as the only method a group of concerned citizens had to guarantee clean drinking water. After exhausting other avenues, the residents of what is now Dover pulled together—and incorporated—in order to apply for federal grant money."[29] Shortly after incorporating, the newly formed city reapplied for the Community Development Block Grant and Farmers Home Administration (FmHA) funding. By Christmas 1988 residents would again learn that they had been turned down for the block grant and would spend at least another two years without clean water—a year for the reapplication process, and a year to complete the water system. The reason the DOC gave for rejecting the application hadn't changed: since the community hadn't yet learned if they would receive FmHA funding, the DOC did not have evidence that they could complete the project. As if to add insult to injury, the project manager for the DOC is quoted as saying that other than lacking the necessary loan, it was "otherwise . . . a very good project."[30]

At Christmas 1989, after another long year without drinkable water and after learning the mill would be indefinitely closed, the city council finally heard the news they had been waiting for: they had been awarded FmHA funding. The FmHA had deemed their project so essential that it covered nearly the entire cost of the project. They were helped in part by FmHA requirements, including a provision that the community be at least 50 percent low- to medium-income; in Dover, nearly 60 percent of the homes qualified. When the paperwork was finalized, the City of Dover received a $569,100 grant and a $193,700 loan from the FmHA to construct the new water system, with voters passing a bond for $214,000 to cover the costs of the loan.[31]

Throughout the process of applying for grants, incorporating the city, and reapplying for grants, residents remained under a boil order and suffered frequent water outages. When the water was running, knowing that it could fail again at any time, residents "filled bathtubs and five-gallon buckets for washing dishes and to flush the toilet." Patty Worth, who owned Dover Daycare and was now also a city councilwoman, had resorted to catching rainwater at her house so she could flush toilets.[32] James Walker was also elected a city councilor and, as a reward, continued to spend entire days "bailing some seven feet of water out of a pump house to get to the submerged motorized unit" to provide "temporarily" running water to Dover residents.[33]

June Griffith, who would later go on to serve on the city council, was raising her family and remembered, "We hauled the water. We . . . went to the old depot in Sandpoint and brought it home." Even when they weren't hauling water, Griffith recalled the challenges she faced: "We could bathe with the water, but . . . then there was such a shortage of water. In the summer, we couldn't water our gardens." Worth described citizens who were "'desperate and irate' in their search for water for drinking, washing dishes, and bathing."[34]

These problems were compounded by other problems. Residents were tethered to their homes, because it became nearly impossible to move during this time. The housing market in Dover was nonexistent. No one could sell a house that did not have clean water. And then the mill closed for good in 1989, making their homes even less valuable. Like many communities in the region, the mill closing was a painful emotional and financial blow, but for Dover, it was yet another problem that added to a growing list of problems the community faced.

Despite hopes that the water system would be up and running by the fall of 1990, a year after they received their FmHA funding, the project suffered a series of setbacks. Instead of clean water, at the end of 1990 residents received yet another water bill from Shamrock Investment Company.[35] It is easy to imagine this bill arriving in the mail and the recipient not having any running water. Additionally, the final six months of 1990 were particularly difficult. The *Daily Bee* reported water outages occurring several times every month, lasting for days on end.[36] And, of course, like the previous five years, it is certain that even if the water happened to be running on that day, whoever received their bill couldn't turn on the faucet for a drink without risking illness.

Finally, in November 1991, Dover's new water system went online. Residents received triumphant letters from the city letting them know "the water is on!" Behind the scenes, the city council had worked tirelessly to see the project through. A month later, Shamrock sent a letter to residents informing them that "effective the date of the letter, Shamrock Investment Company has turned off the [old] water system & will assume no further responsibility to provide water to the residents of Dover."[37]

Of course, now for only the cost of the pipes and hookup fee, Shamrock could hook up to the new water system that the city had been forced to build. Or it could sell the property, which, due to its ceding of responsibility, was now zoned as part of Dover and came with a water system that could be tapped into. In other words, their negligence greatly improved any potential profit on their property. The City of Dover was forced to finance its new water system with a series of federal grants and loans for low-income communities, and now the corporate owners who had refused to update the crumbling water system vastly increased the value of their property thanks to work of the Dover City Council.

UP IN SMOKE

When residents received letters dated December 11, 1991, from Shamrock Investment Company informing them that the company had "turned off the [old] water system & will assume no further responsibility to provide water to the residents of Dover," they understood what it really meant. Shamrock was releasing itself from any legal responsibility to the community. Its claim that it "assumed no further responsibility to provide water" read as ironic, at best, considering that the company had essentially abdicated any responsibility to provide water years earlier.

Once it was freed from legal water woes, Shamrock quickly turned to preparing the site to be sold. The figures likely varied, but the asking price is listed as $5.9 million in news articles detailing the fire that had just decimated the mill.[38] This price, of course, was for a large parcel of waterfront land made more valuable thanks to the new water system.

The company said it planned to salvage what it could from the old mill building, selling the metal for scrap. Publicly, Shamrock said it had no plans to tear down any "historic" buildings, but rumors swirled that everything would be demolished. Patty Worth said she walked down to talk to the men doing the salvage work, who told her directly, "They're pulling the whole thing down." When pressed on the topic by a local reporter on "whether a jumble of derelict wood-frame buildings, overhead steam pipes, and smokestacks might make it difficult to sell a multi-million dollar piece of waterfront," a Shamrock spokesperson had no comment.[39]

The issue of what would become of the old buildings was more than cosmetic. After articles appeared in the paper about the uncertain fate of the site, an anonymous call was made to the Environmental Protection Agency (EPA) in Boise. This led to what "amounted to a stop-work order" on any large-scale demolition at the mill. One of the EPA's primary concerns was the presence of asbestos, but an audit of the property also found "gasoline and diesel spills, solvents, [and] heavy metals" at the site.[40] Soon the Idaho Department of Environmental Quality (DEQ) was involved, taking special note of three buried storage tanks that had never been registered with the agency.

Of course, a little more than two weeks after receiving the news about the stop-work order, many of the questions raised by the residents, the EPA, and the DEQ—like the fate of the historic buildings or the presence of asbestos—would become largely irrelevant.[41]

If anyone held tight to a dream that the mill in Dover would reopen and bring back the jobs that had once helped to sustain a community, it went up in smoke on May 8, 1992. The flames were already shooting twenty feet into the air, ripping through the timber buildings, and engulfing the decades' worth of sawdust by the time firefighters arrived and hooked up to the hydrants. Only after connecting their hoses and attempting to douse the fire did they learn that the hydrants were dry. When Shamrock discontinued water service to the residents of Dover, it also turned off its own water at the mill site. No one had informed the fire department. The morning was unusually windy, and as firefighters raced to find water to battle the flames, it quickly engulfed more and more mill buildings: the stacker, unstacker, planer shed, dry chain, bander shack, shaving shed, and storage shed.[42]

During her lunch break at Sandpoint High School, Nicole Minor saw a plume of smoke rising from Dover. She raced the two and a half miles home to find the entire mill engulfed in fire, with the flames heading toward their homes. Neighbors worked to wet down their roofs with garden hoses, but the fire department had finally hooked up to the city's new water system, which was quickly drained. Out of water yet again, the fire department had to draw directly from the river. Homeowners, however, were left with barely a trickle from their hoses as embers rained down. Ignoring evacuation orders, Dover residents desperately tried to save their homes. As flames came within a hundred yards, people rushed to try and beat them down with tree limbs at the approaching fire line. They knew that if the fire got to the piles of sawdust that buffered the edge of town, some over ten feet deep, it would be unstoppable.[43]

The fire department only stopped the flames by bringing in a bulldozer to build a firebreak between the town and the mill while also dousing the huge expanse of sawdust with water from the river. By the time the day was over, the top two inches of sawdust sat drenched. It was a miracle that no homes were lost, but nearly every building at the mill had burned. Firefighters warned that the sawdust could continue to smolder and pose a fire danger for months to come. They were also forced to fight several additional spot fires for days afterward when the men tasked by Shamrock with watching the site for such an eventuality failed to actually do so.[44]

After eighty-five years, the mill was gone. Mill sites have always been vulnerable to fire, and the Dover mill had a history of them. Remember, the community of Dover only really came into being after a different mill burned downriver and the remaining buildings were relocated. The Dover mill burned in 1928 and didn't reopen until after the Great Depression. And then it burned again in 1945. But by 1992 everyone knew that there would be no rebuilding, no new mill, because, of course, its days had already been numbered.

The fire chief determined that the fire was caused by one of the workers at the site who had been using a cutting torch.[45] Despite the devastation, Shamrock reported that its losses were small, since "most items of value [had already] been removed from the building shells."[46] And, of course, the fire also made moot questions about how to deal with the EPA's concerns about asbestos or whether to preserve some of the historical structures.

CONCLUSION

The fire put an end to Dover's claim to be a timber town. Though work at the mill had become irregular, the mill was always a sort of safety net. It also served as the backdrop to the community for eighty-five years. While a raging inferno that nearly destroyed the entire town was a bit more dramatic of an end than most mills faced, what happened in Dover is a case study of what happened in the American West in that period.

But the loss of a mill is not simply about the loss of a job. It is about the loss of identity and community. Beatrice Adams, who worked as a city clerk in Dover, noted, "You know, nobody back then would have gone to Dover. [Laughter]. It's a mill town. It was a very close-knit mill town. . . . those people that lived in Dover, the people that lived there, the residents, everything they did was as a group, as mill town people. They were very proud of being a mill town." Then she added, thinking about the development that would replace the mill, "This growth: [it] is uneven and unshared."

That sense of community pride was sorely tested throughout the 1980s as the mill owners sought to systematically relieve themselves of all responsibility for the small town of Dover. Since the town's inception, the mill had been the economic life force of Dover, and the residents felt betrayed by the owners' abdication and negligence. The fire burned away all that was left of the old mill and permanently scarred the town's sense of pride, a visceral reminder of the fact that they were on their own. The fire also left behind an expanse of property that the people of Dover felt culturally tied to, thanks to decades of informal use in the heyday of the mill's operations. But while the property owners had abdicated their responsibility for Dover as a community, they certainly hadn't renounced their ownership of the land.

3

Shit Rolls Downhill

Aᴇᴛᴇʀ ᴛʜᴇ ᴍɪʟʟ in Dover burned down in 1992, winter's heavy snows and summer's bleaching sun continued their familiar cycle in Dover. People still talked about the mill like a familiar friend, but mostly only piles of sawdust remained as a reminder of what was. With the mill gone, the quiet in Dover was all around. The familiar hum of the mill was gone and with it the coming and going of trucks.

While the town was suddenly and uncannily still, it was far from quiet for the mayor and the city council, who found that their struggles with infrastructure were only getting started. After over a decade of work to repair and replace the town's decrepit water system, another infrastructure issue was keeping Mayor Marty Jones up at night, often literally: the crumbling bridge on Highway 2 just outside of town. Highway 2 marked the far northern edge of town, dividing old Dover and the mill site from an expanse of forests and sloughs dotted with homes. Running the "back way" between Sandpoint and Spokane, this highway is the only other way into North Idaho if the long bridge crossing Lake Pend Oreille into Sandpoint is closed because of an accident. Following along the Pend Oreille River valley and the route of the old Great Northern Railway, Highway 2 crossed the railroad tracks just to the north of Dover using an old truss bridge.

When chunks of the old bridge would fall away onto the tracks below, leaving gaping holes that looked down onto the railroad tracks, it was Mayor Jones who would get called. He remembered, "Instead of getting ahold of the state, they'd get ahold of me. Here, I'd go up there in the middle of the night . . . and be flagging on that bridge to keep people from falling through these holes." He pointed to the table at which we were sitting, which was probably two and a half feet square, and said that the chucks of the road that were falling from the bridge were as big as the table.

Mayor Jones's wife, Jeannie, was the transportation director for the school district at the time and said she lived in constant fear of hearing that the bridge had collapsed with a busload of kids on it. During the interview, it occurred to me that the bus she was worried about was the one I rode in the 1990s, with Charlie Becker at the wheel and loads of Dover kids filling the green seats.

The mayor and council did everything they could to bring attention to the danger the bridge posed. First, they brought chunks of concrete that had broken off the bridge to the state transportation board. Mayor Jones smiled as he recalled giving those blocks of concrete to each member of the state transportation board as "a souvenir." He and Jeannie said that the board was not impressed, but their stunt did get the attention of the History Channel show *America's Crumbling Infrastructure*, which ran an episode about the bridge. In it, Mayor Jones stands on the bridge pulling chunks of it off as he speaks. The bridge would finally be replaced in 2012, but not before tremendous effort on the part of the entire city council to make it clear that they would fight for their community's safety.

At the same time that the city was fighting to have the bridge replaced, the city of Dover's sewer system was "red-tagged" by the health district, meaning that they couldn't build any additional homes in the community and that contaminated water was being released into the environment. It would seem that the town's infrastructure issues would never cease. After a lengthy fight to fund the new water system (which had been neglected by the mill owners), now the town was stuck between a crumbling bridge and a leaky sewer system.

For the folks in Dover and other rural communities like it, these infrastructure issues were not simply a run of bad luck. The extractive industries that had once brought prosperity to the rural West were changing, and the communities that supported those industries were increasingly obsolete. The crumbling infrastructure of Dover, quite simply, was a product of neglect. The businesses and property owners no longer needed the labor pool that the community of Dover provided, so the town was left to rot, and if not the for the tireless work of the residents, it might just have. The mill owners abdicated responsibility for the water system the mill had provided for decades. The bridge no longer needed to support logging trucks taking the mill's goods to market, so there was no one with the clout to advocate for the decaying roads. And when the town needed a small parcel of land from the unused mill site to repair the unhealthy sewer system, the mill owners extracted a heavy price from the town of Dover to ensure their cooperation. The logging industry in Idaho and across the West was built on government giveaways to the rich and well connected, then sustained on exploitive labor practices, generating massive wealth for large property owners in the region.

The period following the closure of the mills exemplifies Harvey's theory of capital and crises. He argues that after "building of a space for capitalism," those with wealth to invest must "destroy that space (and devalue much of the capital invested therein) at a later point."[1] Only after spaces are effectively devalued can the ruling class return and once again generate profit. In short, to create profit for themselves, the ruling class must constantly reimagine the relationship between labor and space.

This chapter continues to outline what that destruction looks like, as well as the social consequences of that destruction. When timber is no longer as profitable because of the cost of production in the Northwest, the mills and land are devalued, making the people who called it home poorer. The infrastructure of these places—water systems, bridges, sewers—literally breaks down. By leveraging the political and judicial process through highly paid lawyers, developers can reimagine Dover in a way that once again creates capital for the already well-to-do. In this case, a close examination of the back-and-forth between the City of Dover and the development company concerning the city's aging sewer system illustrates the limited measures available to the community to secure their own autonomy. These processes would eventually leave the working people of Dover without access to the spaces that for generations made it what it was.

LOSS AND ANGER IN THE WORKING-CLASS WEST

Dover, of course, was not the only community experiencing rapid loss and change in this period. Across the American West, working-class people were left reeling. The farm crisis of the 1980s was marked by high numbers of foreclosures. It yielded "sad stories of farm sales, farmers taking their own lives, even taking the lives of bankers—all bringing grim reality to this largest farm crisis since the Great Depression."[2] In mining communities and timber communities, meanwhile, particularly in the American West, workers in these industries were replaced by machines that never demand collective bargaining rights. The reverberation of these changes was felt across communities. As paychecks from the mill or the mine quit coming in, other businesses in those communities closed behind them.

As working-class jobs declined in North Idaho, the region became best known for the disproportionate number of antigovernment and white supremacist organizations that sought shelter in the wilderness. In 1992, the Ruby Ridge standoff kept North Idaho in the headlines for weeks after Randy Weaver and his family held federal agents at bay for eleven days. The standoff ended after Weaver's wife and son and a federal agent were killed. Forty miles to the south, the Aryan Nations, led by Richard Butler, built its national headquarters on a twenty-acre property. Butler had grown up in Los Angeles and moved his family to North Idaho in the 1970s to build his compound. The group held marches in their uniforms down the streets of little towns throughout North Idaho. In 1986 an affiliated group robbed banks and blew up a priest's home—because he was the head of a human rights task force—and generally terrorized the region.[3] One of my first memories after moving to Sandpoint in the early 1990s was of members of the Aryan Nations handing out a comic book titled *The Holohoax*—which claimed that the Holocaust was a hoax—outside the high school as we waited for the afternoon bus. I lost count of the number of times their flyers showed up in our mailbox.

Mark Fuhrman would become North Idaho's most infamous resident in 1995. A former LAPD detective, he became a household name during the O. J. Simpson trial, when a recording of him using racial epithets against Black people was made public, bolstering the claim made by Simpson's defense that he was the target of racist white police officers. When the dust from the trial settled, Fuhrman retired from the LAPD and moved to Sandpoint, prompting a 1995 *Spokesman-Review* article, "Many Ex-California Cops Retire to Idaho." These officers were interested in North Idaho not just for the price of land, the article implies, but because they were seeking out white communities that tolerated racial intolerance. In the article, a former LAPD officer seems to affirm this point, even while trying to deny it: "The insinuation that because an LA policeman is moving to Idaho means he's a racist and a bigot cuts me to the soul," the officer said. Instead, "we are here because we are tired of gangs, traffic, and crowds," evoking the imagery of racial and ethnic gangs in order to demonize Los Angeles while celebrating white North Idaho.[4] This cultural and economic background informed the tensions in Dover in the 1990s: as the disinvestment in rural communities combined with increasing racial resentments in the culture more broadly, fringe groups settled in.

This disinvestment meant that Dover faced a failing water system, a leaky sewer system, and a bridge believed by residents to be on the verge of collapse. At the same time, the region faced an influx of new residents drawn by values that were, at the very least, not conducive to building warm and welcoming communities. While Dover grappled with questions around infrastructure and development, North Idaho was fast becoming a hotbed of racism and radical, antigovernment sentiment, making it hard for many North Idaho communities to attract and retain residents. Changes were taking place all around Dover, adding an element of desperation to the town's attempts to save itself.

UNANSWERED QUESTIONS

Against this backdrop of economic and cultural decline in the region, I had assumed that the decision by the Dover City Council to allow for the development of the old mill site would have been made out of economic desperation. The city council records from the period show that the town's budget was constantly in peril, and increasing tax revenues seemed unlikely for a small town with infrastructure problems in a region with a national reputation for antigovernment standoffs and white supremacists. Surely, the decision to develop the property and expand the town had been made after years of lobbying on the part of Shamrock Investment Company, the owners of the property.[5] I imagined that the mill site owners had persistently worn the city council down as Dover struggled with how to fund the sewer system and the bridge, making the town vulnerable in their negotiations with the developer.

But what I found instead was silence. The two groups, the City of Dover and Shamrock Investment Company, had almost no contact—or at least no contact that exists in the public record—for nearly four years after the fire. This silence is unprecedented, given the recent struggles with the water system and the long-standing relationship between the mill and the community. After sifting through years' worth of public records—each year in a heaving manila envelope with the year scribbled in Sharpie across the top, I found instead that while city officials were busy, they weren't busy with issues at the mill site.

After years of day-to-day business and other projects, however, the Dover City Council had a huge attendance roster for its August 1, 1996, meeting, riddled with many names I didn't recognize. There were twice as many people in attendance as usual, including representatives from Shamrock. The meeting seems to have quickly turned to the topic of development: "The discussion went on to the Dover [development] (mill property). The group of men that are represented here tonight would like the council to guarantee the re-zone and try to keep communications open."[6]

Shamrock had seemingly walked into a city council meeting and immediately asked for a guarantee to rezone their property, which would have effectively approved a massive new development. What happened in those years of silence that could have led to such an abrupt proposal being put on the table? What would have led Shamrock to think that it could simply demand a guarantee to rezone based on only a cursory discussion at a single city council meeting?

The minutes from the city council meeting that night are riddled with typos and plenty of misplaced modifiers. After a few readings, however, the conversation seems fairly clear. Shamrock had apparently provided the city with some materials—presumably about having the mill site rezoned—earlier in the year. (If those documents were ever part of the city's official record, they are gone now.[7]) A representative for the developer suggests that "the council re-read the material that was given to the council back in April." A councilor, cutting to the chase, responds by asking one of the developers "why they hadn't filed an application for this property" (presumably an application to have it rezoned). The developer responds by claiming that the application had yet to be filed because "they don't want the council to deny it outright." Not one to mince words, city council member Patty Worth says that "it sounds like they [the developer] want all the guarantees up front." Once she made her disapproval clear, other councilors lined up behind her. The minutes state that one city councilor "would like to see a [timeline] on this project" and another notes, "We have other things that need to be done, [i.e.,] sewer, expansion of water, etc., that need to be dealt with first."[8]

The block of text that summarizes the meeting is chock-full of details but also ambiguity, especially regarding the repeated use of the pronoun "they," which could either mean the city or the developer: "They want to go fast and help with the sewer, but the questions that need to be answered are density, the return of the beach for the citizens of Dover. It was suggested that when this meeting takes place that they come prepared. It was also suggested that it be in the form of a public hearing. There was some discussion to the fact that Dover Development will give the land to the sewer but they want a guarantee for contract zoning, expansion when needed of the sewer, and water."[9]

By the time I read these documents, sitting at a long table at the newly built Dover City Hall, watching birds coming and going from my riverfront view, I thought I had a reliable timeline of events around the Mill Lake development. I had interviewed dozens of key players in the decision and read more than a decade's worth of local and regional newspaper articles about Dover, in addition to having conducted archival research at the Bonner County Historical Society. With my timeline in place, I thought that the city council records would simply help me understand *why* the City of Dover had eventually agreed to rezone the property when there was significant pressure from the community not to do so.

Instead of pulling all the threads of my research together, the at times incomplete notes from the city council raised more questions than they answered. It simply didn't seem possible that the first mention of the development would start with a "guarantee [to] re-zone."

It became clear that the timeline I had built was not complete, and that many of the people I interviewed—including city councilors and former mayors—might not even have a complete picture of the complex processes that led up to that August 1, 1996, meeting.

I started in earnest to understand what I had overlooked by reexamining the records from the beginning of the city's existence, looking for these new names to show up in attendance records, or for any other hints based on that single entry. It became clear that while the city kept careful notes of the pressing local issues it was wrestling with—how to keep the roads passable, how to keep the water running and bills paid—there simply were not city council records that discussed zoning and development before the August 1, 1996, meeting. Instead, the city council notes showed it addressing day-to-day issues, like a yard that "looks real messy" (the councilors decided that the best course of action, in this case, was to talk to the man's "mother and drop some hints").

One thing, however, did become clear as I gained more insight into the timeline of events. The City of Dover and Shamrock were brought into conflict in the years after the fire destroyed the mill by one key issue that would give the developers leverage: the sewers.

LEAKY SEWERS

The sewer system's issues had been bad for some time, but by the summer of 1991, the health district reported sewage surfacing in Dover's drain field. Residents all had individual septic tanks, but those tanks connected to this single drain field: a series of perforated pipes buried two feet deep and sandwiched in a foot of gravel. In a working system, the wastewater travels into the pipes and seeps out at the perforations, moving through the gravel layer and into the soil around it. The soil acts as a filter for the wastewater until it is mostly clean and ends up absorbed by the plants above it. Unfortunately, the soil in Dover has a higher-than-average level of silt (until the end of the Ice Age, it had been the bed of a giant lake). This silt then clogged the layer between the drainage gravel and soil above it. The wastewater, unable to be absorbed into the soil, could only build up. Eventually, a wet period would saturate the soil and allow the sewage to flood to the surface, posing obvious environmental and health issues for the community.

Because the sewer system predated the city of Dover, it was operated by an independent board: the Rocky Point Sewer District. Ninety percent of the system, however, fell within the city limits of Dover, and a number of the sewer board members were also Dover city councilors.[10] The failure of the sewer system was dire for the community, and it also meant that state regulators stopped the district from adding any homes to the system so as not to add to the sewage problems. This made any growth in the area simply impossible. It was this stipulation that likely got the attention of Shamrock Investment Company. Even if it could get its property rezoned for development, it is very difficult to sell high-end homes that lack toilets.

There is a certain irony that sewage would set in motion a series of events that would forever alter the town. Yet, it was a problem that had to be fixed. The obvious solution was to simply take the homes in the Rocky Point Sewer District and connect them to the city of Sandpoint's sewer system. Sandpoint had plenty of capacity and even briefly envisioned building a larger plant and moving it out of town (its sewage plant currently sits lakeside, next to the high school football stadium—what must be one of the most scenic waste treatment plants in the country). Connecting to the Sandpoint system was the solution that the DEQ recommended, and it was also the most cost efficient, though Dover residents did worry about being forced to pay Sandpoint property taxes, because the cost of its brand-new sewer system was considerable. Furthermore, since the old system's drain field had failed prematurely, they would still be paying on that system as well.[11]

After much debate and a split decision, the City of Sandpoint agreed to the request to let the Rocky Point Sewer District connect to the Sandpoint system, but it set a condition: Sandpoint would take the sewage, but it would also take the city of Dover.[12] In other words, either Dover agreed to be annexed by Sandpoint or it would be faced, once again, with finding funding to undertake a huge public works project with a tiny city budget. Undeterred, Dover chose the latter.

For the immediate past mayor, Kate Morris, who, two decades later, still spent most of her time dealing with sewer issues, the decision was vexing. "Way back," she said, "I would've made the decision to [be annexed by] Sandpoint. Think of the money and headaches that all of this could've avoided." Even some who had lived in Dover during the annexation decision disagreed with it. Evan Johnson, who had moved to Dover nearly forty years earlier, noted, "They always say, you know, it's more expensive to brush and flush in Dover than anywhere . . . They were stubborn. They didn't want anything to do with Sandpoint."

For residents who were born in Dover, the decision may not have been easy, but the alternative was unthinkable. There had always been a long-standing rivalry between Dover and Sandpoint, between the working-class Dover kids and their more affluent neighbors. Beatrice Adams remembers her ex-husband explaining to her that "it was kind of like the kids in Sandpoint were the 'townies,' and the kids from Dover were the 'mill kids,' and the kids from Sagle were the 'farm kids.' They always had a tag, right from the very beginning. Of course, the townies were top of the heap."

It may have been a sort of one-sided rivalry by the 1990s. Dover kids had been bused into Sandpoint schools for a generation, and Dover was only one of the smaller dozen or so little towns in Sandpoint's orbit. However, for folks who could remember the school in Dover, who grew up playing on the River Rats baseball team, and who had fought so hard to incorporate the town in order to save it, it was simply unthinkable to be swallowed up by Sandpoint over a little raw sewage. As Tim Casten put it, "I live in Dover. And my description of Dover is: I live in Dover, Idaho. Sandpoint is a suburb of Dover."

The city council estimated that 90 percent of Dover residents would oppose the annexation.[13] Clarence Hill remembers when the city wrestled with the decision. "They just had a town growing, and they didn't like Sandpoint," Hill said. "Maybe when [Sandpoint] tried to annex the whole deal, that might have kind of woke 'em up a little bit. They came along, and they supported something. They didn't want to be part of Sandpoint."

Larry Davis remembers it the same way, saying, "[Sandpoint] had just kind of [made] up some bossy, dictatorial policies, and statements, about how 'We're takin' over. You're gonna get what you're gonna get. We're the boss. Don't ask questions. Just keep outta the way.' It was just an attitude like that."

And so, much like they had done with their water system, the community resolved to fix the sewer problem themselves. The first step was a decision so unprecedented that the chairman of the sewer district described it as "plowing fresh, untouched snow."[14] The City of Dover and the Rocky Point Sewer District decided to dissolve the sewer district and have the City of Dover absorb it. While there was no precedent—officials could not find a single example of a city taking over a sewer or water district—the process appears to have gone smoothly. After a 70–14 vote of approval from Dover residents, the City of Dover officially acquired the Rocky Point Sewer District in the summer of 1996 and added sewage to its list of responsibilities.[15]

The first issue was securing funding to repair the broken system they had just agreed to take over. The sewer system had been projected to cost $800,000 when discussions began in 1991, but by the time the plans were finalized in 1995, it came with a $1,032,000 price tag. The transfer had been in the works for years, and many city councilors were also on the sewer district's board, so grant writing to fund the project had been happening for some time before the takeover. By the time Dover was officially responsible for the sewers, most of the funds to pay for the new system had already been raised. Specifically, they had secured four separate US Department of Agriculture grants totaling over half a million dollars and a Department of Commence grant for another half a million dollars in only a few years. They had gotten pretty good at writing infrastructure grants.[16]

However, even with the million-dollar price tag to rebuild the sewer system raised, the city still did not have anywhere to put a sewage plant or the money to buy the land to put it on.[17] The most obvious solution was to build the plant on the old mill site. So in the months before the sewers were transferred to Dover, the city government hired an attorney, Paul Clark, to write a letter to the "partners of Dover Development" (Shamrock) informing them that to build its sewer system, the city needed to acquire 12.49 acres of the old mill property. In the letter,

Shamrock was informed that the city had taken the liberty of having the property appraised and that they were ready to pay the $85,000 appraised value. Because the city could not use grants to pay for this land, the residents would be left to fund the $85,000 through bonds, meaning that the city could not afford to pay any more for the land. In what surely added insult to injury, Dover's attorney included a copy of a pamphlet titled "When a Public Agency Acquires Your Property" with the letter.[18]

Purchasing the land from the mill site owners had always been part of the city's plan after it acquired the old Rocky Point Sewer District, but the city councilors probably did not anticipate that this purchase would become a source of contention with Shamrock, and that the ensuing legal battles with the owners would later tie their hands concerning a new development in their town.

ZONING AND LEGAL BATTLES

What happened among the Rocky Point Sewer District, Shamrock, and the City of Dover is mostly lost to history—or at least remains only in the memories of people who are not talking. Instead, we are left with puzzle pieces: a public workshop without any corresponding paperwork, response letters without the letter that prompted them, and court documents where legalistic language obscures motivations. What must be true is that Shamrock and the City of Dover had been communicating since at least the spring of 1996, but likely much earlier than that, given the numerous references to an April 4, 1996, workshop.

Piecing together the record, however, reveals that Shamrock had no intention of simply selling the requested parcel of land so that the city of Dover could use its grant money to build a new sewer system. While the record of conversations between the city and the developer is incomplete, it does show that Shamrock and Mayor Jones had been engaged in a discussion around the sale of the land in 1996. The mill site owners, it seemed, would only sell the land to the city on the condition that the remaining land was rezoned to allow them to develop it.

The city's own letters imply that—before getting the advice of an attorney—the city thought it could work directly with a development company to reach some kind of compromise around the land it needed for the sewer system. And it was anxious to reach that compromise, because the fate of the grants it had secured for the sewer system hung in the balance. The million dollars that had been raised needed to be applied toward a project quickly or else the city risked losing the funds. In written exchanges between Shamrock's attorney and Mayor Jones, however, the mayor informs the attorney that it is not legal to work out an agreement with Shamrock without public hearings.[19]

Jones, while new to serving as mayor and desperate to get the sewer up and running, nevertheless appears stalwart in his attempts to uphold the law. He wrote: "We ask that Dover Development [Shamrock] and its legal representatives, clearly understand the determination of the City of Dover to resolve the current sewer issues with the best consideration for all residents. However, the determination will not allow for agreements that serve to circumvent zoning processes." Jones continued: "We believe and have received legal counsel that to 'work out an agreement' regarding Dover Development's zoning proposal prior to the application and public hearing process would be inappropriate."[20]

After sending the letter, the city quickly scheduled a public hearing to discuss rezoning the property. The minutes from that September 24, 1996, meeting suggest that residents were not planning to give any concessions to the developers. After a group of residents asked what would happen to "the beach," one of the developers told them it was "non-negotiable": it would be sold. After that, the list of major concerns generated by residents included not only the beach but also utilities, schools, roads, and density. By the end of the evening, not a single resident spoke in favor of the contract zoning that the developers had requested (a type of zoning that would have created a contract between the city and the developers wherein the developer agrees to certain conditions in exchange for a zoning treatment they would largely design). Instead, they told councilors to "stick to their guns" and not allow contract zoning.[21]

People who witnessed these meetings with Shamrock remembered trying to use whatever power they had in these processes, including small power plays to show the development representatives that the town wouldn't be intimidated. One former city official, for example, remembered forcing the development representatives in their business suits to take a pizza break before their section of the meeting would commence.

3.1. The old "sandy beach," where generations of Doverites learned to swim. To the right, the edge of the bluff meets the water. For many years the beach sat behind a "no trespassing" sign; today a multimillion-dollar home obscures the view of the lake from the road.

"They came in after our regular meeting," he said. "We'd wanted to take a break. They [felt] quite important, and they really didn't want [there] to be a break, because they wanted to get home, go do whatever they were going to do with their families. I ordered pizza. . . . City council and everybody that was there from the city, we all ate pizza. Of course, that was a little, probably below them, under them, eating pizza. After we got done having pizza, then we met with them."

Frustrated with the town's refusal to consider rezoning for development, one of the developers shot back, "We could sell this property off to a bunch of litigious sharks tomorrow, and where would you be?"[22] This threat, reported in a newspaper article, is the only one that exists in the record, but it fits the memories of citizens and council members who felt that they were held hostage, particularly to the prospect of turning Dover into a gated community where outside residents would be locked out from having access to the water. In eight separate interviews, residents remember that very early on a group of men came in and threatened to turn the mill site into a gated community, something the residents vehemently opposed. There is not a single written document that refers to this threat, but the consistency with which the old-timers remembered hearing it suggests that it was probably made in one of the early meetings.

Importantly, this threat of a gated community is what led many people to accept the idea of development at all, as a different kind of development became the lesser of two evils for the community. Evan Johnson remembered, "We were averse to a gated community. It's almost inconceivable to live in Dover and think of a gated community."

After the contentious public hearing in September, the city's attorney again responded to the developers, telling them that the city was simply not in a position to rezone the property before they needed to take possession of the acreage for the sewer plant.[23] We can't know how Shamrock responded, but shortly afterward Mayor Jones wrote yet another letter to the developers and told them that what they were asking for—a guarantee to rezone in exchange for the property to build the sewer—is against the law. Jones's letter implies that the city may have done some wheeling and dealing before it brought in an attorney and that it was not at all opposed to seeing the site developed, but that it had to follow procedures.[24]

The response from Shamrock was swift: either rezone or see us in court. They also sweetened the deal for the city: offering the land for the sewer plant at no cost if the city promised to rezone. But if the city refused to rezone, Shamrock would increase the price tag for the land to $1.3 million.[25]

Weeks later, they were in court, at which point the City of Dover and Shamrock reached a settlement whereby the city promised to try to rezone the property by April 1, 1997. In exchange, they could purchase the land for the sewer for $85,000. The stipulation also noted that the new sewer system had to service at least six hundred households (in other words, it had to be big enough for the development Shamrock wanted to build) and that the city would rezone the land to increase density and then not rezone it for ten years, provided that the developers promised not to sell it during that period. The stipulation also required that the city pass a municipal ordinance authorizing planned unit developments (PUDs), which would permit multiple uses, including residential, multi-family, and commercial.[26]

Mayor Jones remembered the challenges associated with that time. "We had great battles with the state over [the sewer]," he said, "because they would only allow you to build a system that would take care of the people that lived there at that point in time. At the same time we were dealing with that, [Shamrock] was coming and wanting to get this developed. We finally got the state to OK the idea of building the sewer plant that's across here, and then we could add to it later on different units to be able to use through the same sewer plan."

By May of 1997, the city and the developers each met their obligations. A public hearing on March 18, 1997, amended the zoning ordinance to allow, by special-use permit, a PUD on the old mill site. (The notes from the meeting are missing, so it's unclear if anyone showed up to oppose it or what they might have said.) On April 22, the next public hearing was held first to rezone the mill site from agricultural to residential use and to then allow that newly rezoned residential land to be organized using PUD zoning. In other words, the city carefully but quickly took the required steps to allow the entire mill site to be developed as a cohesive development by one group, meaning that it would be less likely that separate subdivisions would pop up on the site and more likely be something that might add to the community feel of Dover.

But the minutes from this meeting are missing too. The only records of either public meeting are notices in the newspaper.[27] I should note that, in general, the city's records are very well kept. They are arranged by year, each year in individual folders, with the material inside organized in chronological order. Each item in the folder includes a dated agenda followed by the notes from that particular meeting. Because meetings tended to follow reliable timelines (they were most often biweekly on Tuesdays), it is easy to use a calendar and check off each meeting. In other words, I feel confident in saying that the notes that are missing are specifically related to public hearings about the development. The meetings clearly happened, as their agendas remained neatly in place, but any notes are gone. And the tapes with recordings of these meetings, carefully labeled in a large box labeled "Dover Development," are all blank. The transcriptions of the tapes that the former city clerk remembers organizing? They are all gone too.

I spent months transfixed on the mystery of it all, wishing that my fancy degree had prepared me to also make sense of it. But while I have plenty of conjectures, I am trained not to guess but to make sense of the world using the evidence I have.

CONCLUSION

My project started with a simple question: Why was Dover rezoned and a development eventually approved? But in my interviews, no one could answer that question. To be fair, many of the people best suited to answering it—those who had served on the city council at the time—had passed away in the intervening years. Nevertheless, no one else could or would answer the question. My interviews had painted a vibrant picture of life in Dover across the decades, but no one could explain the mechanisms that led to the development that would alter the town so significantly. This lack of clarity, combined with the general chaos in Dover—including the boil order, the mill closing, the mill burning down, and the sewer failing—meant I didn't expect to find a simple explanation.

But once all the old newspapers, letters, and council minutes were lined up, they told a clear and concise story: the city was no match for the mill owners' lawyers. By the time the developers showed up in Dover in August of 1996, demanding their property be rezoned, the community was in the midst of significant economic upheaval and several infrastructure crises. This meant that the few low-income town residents simply couldn't afford the kind of robust legal representation that would effectively advocate for their rights to determine the future of their community in the face of wealthy developers who wanted to profit from the land. And they knew it. When I asked someone who had been on the city council what they would recommend to a community facing a similar situation, the answer was simple: immediately hire the very best lawyer you can afford.

That the mechanism for rezoning in Dover was clear and legal, however, does not make it just. It was the mill site owners who had left the city without drinkable water. It was those same owners who allowed the city to use grants for low-income communities to fix that issue, knowing that once Dover had built the water infrastructure, the mill site property was considerably more valuable. Then, amid the sewer crisis, the city asked to buy 12.49 acres from those same property owners at the appraised value, so the city would have a place to build a working sewer system for the community. Even though the sewer system, like the water system before it, would make the mill site even more valuable, the property owners knew that they could not profit from the land without getting the city to rezone it. So they used the failing sewer system as leverage to force the city's hand on zoning, backed by the courts. The new sewer system built in the wake of this deal was also funded by federal grants designed for low-income communities. Once the new water and sewer systems were in place, the mill site owners turned around and sold the newly rezoned property to Mill Lake Development, raking in a tidy profit.

In other words, the former mill owners saw huge financial gains precisely *because* they failed to provide drinkable water to the people of Dover and *because* they refused to aid in solving the town's sewage crisis. Shamrock abdicated all responsibility for the community, allowing the town's infrastructure to crumble to the point that required massive federal grants for low-income communities. As a reward for their negligence, the mill site owners sold their now-valuable property for millions. Large properties such as the mill site were essentially given by the federal government to large corporations in the nineteenth century, and now its owners were profiting off the labor and suffering of the community, bankrolled by federal grants. Shamrock realized huge profits because a low-income community provided *them* with plenty of clean water, a sewer system, and PUD zoning.

The injustice of these arrangements would mostly be hidden from public scrutiny—many of the Dover residents I spoke to did not seem to know much about the contested negotiations over the sewer system, which were largely conducted by the mayor, the city council, and the developer. Additionally, plans to develop the old mill site moved slowly after the 1997 rezoning of the property, leading many residents to assume that there weren't any plans in the works and that the city still retained the power to reject specific development proposals that might come along. Moreover, the grants that Dover received to build the new sewer system came with severe restrictions—the city couldn't add new homes to the sewer system if they were built on the hundred-year floodplain, as much of the old mill site was. The issue of development seemed to have dissipated for most folks in Dover.

The floodplain issue led Shamrock to give up its plans to develop the property and instead look for a new buyer (who would have to find a way around these regulations). When that new developer came along with plans for the mill site in 2003, many Dover residents would again agitate against the idea of transforming the town. But with the 1997 rezoning now just a fuzzy memory, this new resistance to development couldn't understand why all the avenues of legal opposition seem to have evaporated.

4

It's ~~Not~~ Over in Dover

T HE STORY OF Dover is populated by characters who illustrate the divisions between the old and the new American West. The mayor who oversaw the Mill Lake development vote, Marty Jones, raises livestock and favors coveralls and a cowboy hat. Marty and Jeannie Jones call a cozy log house home. It overlooks their pastureland and the long driveway that winds from the main road up to their house, which sits nestled on a hillside on the land Jeannie's family has farmed for generations. It is filled with all the trappings of a busy farm life, including an array of working dogs and very friendly cats who came and went throughout our interview.

In 2014, after the development was put in and only days after his barn was destroyed by a fire that killed many of his sheep, Mayor Jones stepped down after nearly twenty years of leading the community. The new mayor, who was appointed to fill his seat, Kate Morris, brought with her a more formal tone to Dover, and it seemed appropriate that she would invite me to meet her at the new Dover City Hall, where the challenges of running a city that had nearly doubled in size—and all the sewage it generated—fell to her. Morris had moved to the area nearly twenty years earlier when she and her husband decided to make their vacation/retirement home their permanent one. Before becoming mayor, she'd lived in New York, Philadelphia, and Chicago, working for advertising agencies and biotech companies. Her lakefront house in the Mill Lake development is built on the bluff facing the water and where she is now busy raising twin daughters. It is where Jones's wife grew up riding her horses, a once quasi-public space shared by the community that is unquestionably now "private property."

Dover, then, offers a story about change in a once-thriving timber community that is familiar to many towns in the Pacific Northwest. But Dover's story is also unique to this community, its citizens, and its quirks. It is the story of missing city council minutes and blank tapes about the development. Depending on whom you ask, it's the story of a "local boy" making good by developing Dover and finally giving the community an official beach and public trails. Or maybe it's the story of a local bully who threatened anyone who opposed him and then reneged on the promises he made to the overly trusting residents.

This chapter explores the resistance to the development in the face of these competing narratives. Unsure about who had the power to slow down or stop the development, a group of Dover residents attempted to build a campaign against what they saw as a corporate, hostile takeover of their quaint community. Assured that the law was on their side, based on their understanding of the zoning regulations, these residents were disheartened to find that no strategy seemed capable of questioning the legal standing of the development. Every avenue seemed futile, and in the face of that futility, one story, in particular, seemed to gain traction: the owner and public face of the new development, Don Wilson, despite his ties to the community, was a ruthless negotiator who would push the law or intimidate his opponents to get what he wanted. As Dover residents tried to grapple with the complex legal realities of the development, even those who begrudgingly supported it seemed sure that Wilson's tactics bulldozed the opposition.

In all my research, I never found any evidence that Wilson broke the law. That so many Dover residents focused on issues of legality as the reason that the development was approved, however, indicates that the process of development felt confusing and unfair. The complexity of this story made it nearly impossible for even those immersed in the debate to totally understand it. Thus, when the system of byzantine rules that organized the development never seemed to err on the side of those who opposed the development, it seemed logical for opponents to direct hostilities at a public figure rather than at the legal and political structures that disempowered them.

There are numerous examples in this chapter of how the developer was able to avoid some of the laws and regulations seemingly designed to protect the environment or community interests. In one example, the developer carefully (but legally) avoided rules limiting the number of acres of wetlands that can be filled in as part of a construction project, then individual Mill Lake landowners filled in small sections of wetlands on their properties, which is believed to have flooded a horse pasture upstream from the development. The person who owns that horse pasture—which now has a wetland in it that cannot be filled—has essentially no legal recourse.

Ultimately, communities like Dover have very little power against the individual legal rights of those with economic might. This is certainly by design. In the introduction, I applied Harvey's theory of the spatial fix to Dover, showing how it—and North Idaho more generally—was "built" as a space for capitalist accumulation. But building a space for capitalism is more than laying railroad tracks and erecting mills; it means creating a network of laws that protect whatever industry has economic clout and it makes the laws that support their efforts appear natural and inevitable.

Under this system, the mill owner's rights superseded the mill workers' rights, and mill owners would use this power—legal, political, economic, and even military—to maintain their control. That the narrative in Dover became one about a single bad actor suggests just how effective this system has been internalized in and obscured from people in these communities. While some of the developer's actions certainly opened him up to this kind of criticism, critiquing him as an individual effectively allows the larger economic, legal, and political system he worked within to operate unchanged. The rumors and vitriol around the developer suggest just how powerless people feel against this system, even when they do understand it.

RESISTING THE DEVELOPMENT

In a laundry list of important dates for Dover, September 2, 2004, stands out. On this day, the Dover City Council, made up of Marty Jones and other longtime, working-class city councilors, voted 3–1 to approve the plans for the new Mill Lake development. The vote meant that three hundred acres of the old mill site would become a "600-unit upscale development." Like other key documents relating to the development, the minutes from this meeting are missing. Only a short agenda remains in the public records. The tapes used to record the meeting are blank. Their transcriptions are also missing, but the newspaper article about the evening reports one opponent "moved to tears" and another ripping a pile of pamphlets touting the proposed development to shreds. The tears and the dramatically destroyed documents conveyed the sense of injustice felt by opponents who had tirelessly fought the development.

Some of their anger stemmed from the speed of the process. The first public hearing on the Mill Lake development happened in December 2003, less than a year before its approval. In that period, opponents frantically tried every tool imaginable to stop the development: attending meetings, writing letters to the editor, contacting state and federal agencies, and even hiring a lawyer.

It wasn't just that the process had moved rapidly. It had also completely blindsided them. Lindsey Green, a schoolteacher at the time who would go on to fight against the development, only learned that the land was likely going to be developed while building her modest 1,089-square-foot home to replace the "ailing double-wide" that she had called home. Toward the end of the project, she was chatting with her builder, looking over the vast expanse of land right outside her front door. During their conversation, she said to him, "This is going to stay a wetland for all of perpetuity, forever," because of the conditions of the loan given to the city. He looked over and told her, "Oh, Lindsey, no, it's not," explaining that Don Wilson was trying to build a development on that land.

Green and many of her neighbors believed that the old mill site was undevelopable because of "the loan," shorthand for the numerous USDA and other federal grants the city had used to build the new sewer system. These grants seemingly restricted building within the hundred-year flood zone. Since much of the mill site was in that zone, their understanding was well founded. The restrictions were clear and meant that the funding to replace the city's infrastructure limited the scope of any future development.

However, many residents were unaware that the city had been forced by the courts to rezone the mill site in May of 1997 in exchange for 12.49 acres to build the town's new sewer system. And even fewer realized the significant power this particular type of zoning—"planned use development"—gave any future developer, especially in Idaho, over what they could do to the land.

If there was pushback in those rezoning meetings in May of 1997, we will never know. From a records standpoint, only the results of those meetings exist, but the meetings themselves left no documentary evidence. The files for the meetings before and after that meeting—in which the city council debated how to inform residents that their yards needed some tidying or the roads needed a bit more gravel—sit carefully in their manila envelopes labeled with the month and year. But the records for the meeting that had essentially decided the development issue for the town only exists in a tiny notice in the newspaper. The concrete results of that meeting, however, are the roads that etch their way across the old mill site, past the marina, and around the condos: the development itself. In essence, when the city rezoned the property in 1997 as a PUD, they essentially okayed the development in Dover. The city council could vote a particular plan up or down with cause, but it no longer had control over *if* a development would happen.

Green and others, however, felt protected from any development because of a second court ruling that seemed to limit the scope of building in the area. In 1998, the city and Shamrock faced a final court date, when the developers discovered that the USDA grant money—"the loan" that the city was using to fund the sewer system—included stipulations that would limit the size of any development. The USDA funding specifically prohibited homes built within the hundred-year floodplain from accessing sewer services. Since about half of the development had been planned for this flood zone, it dramatically limited the number of homes that could be built. Ultimately, the judge ruled in favor of the city, believing it had operated in good faith when it made the agreement.[1] This meant that the city could not approve any development that included homes in the floodplain without having to repay the hundreds of thousands of dollars in grant money.

After this ruling, the trail of documents about the mill site being developed goes cold for nearly five years. Many residents understandably believed that this ruling essentially kept the land from being developed, and the relative quiet about a development cemented that belief. In essence, when Green shared with her builder that the land would stay wetland forever, she was right. What she and others couldn't know was that the developer would agree to pay off some of the USDA grants to get around these limitations on building in the hundred-year flood zone.

It is no surprise that Green's name shows up on the list of people at the first public hearing about the development. She became part of a loosely organized group of residents who strongly opposed the development, including Lee Bell, Garrett Martin, Erica Peterson, Ted Foster, and Iris Sanders, among others. This group of about ten citizens thought they might be able to stop the project, or at least limit the scope of it, and they worked tirelessly to do so.

At the first public hearing to discuss the proposed development in December 2003, over three dozen people showed up to the hearing, with opponents lambasting the proposal as "McDover" or "Doveropolis." Others called the presence of the development a sort of "coup d'état."[2] Almost no residents spoke enthusiastically for the development. Instead, the council's public hearings included three sets of actors: Dover residents opposed to the development, old-timer residents who seemed mostly resigned about the fate of Dover, and the men representing the development.

As the developer worked to get permits from various agencies to build on the site and into the river, residents filed into meetings around the county. Only weeks after the first public hearing in Dover, sixty people showed up at a meeting in Sandpoint where a 274-slip marina for the development was being considered by the Idaho Department of Lands. Of the thirty people who spoke that evening, seventeen voiced opposition, with one calling the development an example of "savage capitalism." Of those who spoke in favor of the development, their support could also be read as a sort of resignation, heard in things like "if we don't plan for growth, it will come piecemeal and it will eat us alive" or that having a planned marina would limit "a series of toothpick docks along the shoreline." Throughout the process, the developer tried to allay concerns by promising residents that his plan would increase public access to the water and that the development would be a cohesive, community-minded project.[3]

Critics continued to make a case against the development in whatever venues they could, becoming fixtures at the city council meetings, writing guest columns in the local paper, and penning numerous letters to the editor. The group even hired a lawyer, who told them they had a strong case, because he believed the City of Dover didn't follow the requirements for a public hearing for the rezoning. However, the lawyer mysteriously quit, telling his clients that he could not represent them but nothing else, only days before the final vote.[4]

In one of her final letters to the editor in December 2004, Erica Peterson, a vocal opponent, implored, "To those of you who insist that there is nothing that we can do and it's going to happen anyway, you might be right. But there is a small group of us that want to slow things down. There's a group of us that love Bonner County and have hope for its future. We must stand up and take responsibility for what will happen."[5]

Despite her efforts and those of others, a decade after the mill burned and the city began discussions with developers, the city officials approved a development plan for the area.[6] Construction of roads for the development started the following spring.

For one opponent, watching the development be built was simply unbearable. After decades in Dover, he moved to a different community. For Lee Bell, likewise, the process left her feeling totally defeated. After all the work they did to slow the development, with very little reward for their efforts, she said that her opposition "did something to my sense of hope that you can make a difference if you use facts." Her efforts only affirmed to her that "you can't win against big money. You just can't win."

In retrospect, the opposition to the development came too late in the process. Looking further back in the timeline by another decade, it seems clear that these opposition efforts were likely doomed years earlier. However, because the rezoning in 1997 happened so quickly and left no records, it is difficult to know what, if any, opposition there was from residents—or if any opposition would have mattered, given the court settlement between the developers and the city.

Sandy Lenn cast the lone opposing vote against the development. She had run a write-in campaign for a position on the Dover city council after news of the development spread. But even as the only holdout, she conceded that the development plan was "consistent with Dover's zoning ordinances." She felt comfortable with her "no" vote, however, because she did "not believe [the development plan] was consistent with the comprehensive plan."[7] Lenn passed away in 2016, but her husband remembers that she wanted to be on the council in part because the development seemed inevitable but she wanted to ensure that the specifics served the community's needs. In remembering the difficulty of the months leading up to the vote, he said it just finally felt like, "Let's make it happen with the least amount of pain. Let's lube it up and make it work."

"LOCAL BOY" OR BULLY?

Lenn's sense of inevitability was generally shared across the old Dover community. Even those who supported the development recognized that there was no stopping it. But few understood that its inevitability was ensured, in part, by the mill owners themselves. As I describe in previous chapters, the mill owners allowed the infrastructure of the community to deteriorate to the point where it was unusable, thus forcing the community into a difficult position: in order to rebuild that infrastructure, the city was legally forced to negotiate with the very people who left them vulnerable in the first place.

Residents were understandably confused about the process, and those who understood felt powerless to resist. Faced with such ambiguities, many in the community turned their attention, and often anger, onto the developer himself, not a legal and political system that makes it easier for those with money (and good lawyers) to exercise exponentially more power than residents. There was neither enough information nor access to information for Dover residents, so the most available explanation was to use the specter of Wilson's money and reputation to make sense of the changes in their community.

Dover residents' confusion about what would happen to the mill site reflects my own experience of sorting through piles of documents and interviews, trying to make sense of them. Residents were confused about nearly all the basic elements of the development—and, frankly, for quite some time so was I. The fact that many documents and records have disappeared only adds to that confusion. Even today, residents who were seemingly neutral during the process continue to debate how the development came to be.

For example, Sarah Walker, who grew up in Dover, said she thought the city owned the mill site at one time. As she explained it: "Dover's funds were low and . . . they were going to sell the mill property because it wasn't a mill anymore. And their best option was to sell it to somebody local." That somebody local was Don Wilson, but Walker said that "locals were generally pissed off about it because it seemed to go against Dover." Her misunderstanding about the mill site's ownership is understandable, given that the site had been a community gathering spot for nearly a century.

Janice Taylor, a retiree who moved to the Mill Lake development soon after it opened, offered a different explanation, but one that suggests that the city had some power to decide who would buy the land. According to Taylor, "There were a lot of people who wanted to come into this lumber mill. Don won the rights supposedly 'cause he, number one, was a hometown boy. Number two, he said he would build the city hall."

Amid these confusing and contradictory stories, Don Wilson's name was synonymous with Mill Lake Development, but not often in a good way. I routinely heard residents say that Wilson must have done something vaguely unethical to gain access to the land. I understood that confusion. I spent nearly two years of my research feeling very unsure about basic elements of the timeline. As noted in an earlier chapter, part of my confusion was the results of being blocked by gatekeepers or being ignored by them. I was left wondering if the unreturned calls and archivists who quit helping when they found out the name of my research site were acts of intentional gatekeeping or simply benign neglect. With the lack of any documentation supporting Wilson's acquisition of the mill site, I thought that maybe the residents' understanding of the process might be accurate, if totally confusing. Perhaps Wilson was simply a front for the real owner, or maybe he was somehow connected to the city in some way.

It was often reported that Wilson had been allowed to develop because he was a "local boy." Wilson's family had lived in the area for generations. He had been a fixture in the larger community for years and was well known in Dover. He had served on the Rocky Point Sewer District board, the board that turned over the sewer system to Dover so they could write grants to repair it, grants that were only available to low-income towns. He had worked at the mill in Dover as a young man and had even played for the Dover River Rats.

Wilson's presence is of key importance, because many residents accepted the process of development, even if begrudgingly. After all, Wilson was a local who they hoped would do right by the community. They had almost no faith in the political system to support them, and even if Wilson was not entirely well liked among residents, he was considered a known entity.

In the 1970s, Wilson had left the area to seek his fortune in the oil fields in Alaska. When he returned to Bonner County, he used that money to begin buying up waterfront land with a sort of clairvoyance for what land would be most valuable. Wilson said he had had an epiphany while having a cup of coffee at a place looking over Prince William Sound in Valdez, Alaska: for the price of a cup of coffee, he could enjoy a million-dollar view. He figured that the shores of Lake Pend Oreille needed similar treatment. Records starting in 1986 show that Wilson and his wife began buying up lakefront property—and lots of it. Their timing was perfect: the region was entrenched in a recession due to the loss of timber jobs, so it was a buyer's market. Still, local people had a hard time believing that the son of a used car salesman could afford the mill site.

Ted Foster, a longtime resident of Dover, articulated a common theory around Wilson's involvement: that he was simply a local front for another, wealthier development company, perhaps even Shamrock, whose plans had been rejected. As Foster explains it, the original mill owners wanted to develop the mill site, but "they were given the stonewall, the blank face, or denied." In response, they, according to Foster's theory, made a deal with Don Wilson, allowing him to develop the property, presumably since he was a local and would be able to get the other residents on board with the development.

This theory was aided by the fact that "the developers" went by so many names, and they were used rather inconsistently. It appears that after the mill closed and burned down, Shamrock Investment Company remained involved, but court documents throughout the 1990s also use the names Dover Development, Dover Enterprises LP, and Dover Development Company, presumably referring to the same group of owners. There is no evidence of Don Wilson ever officially being involved with this group of developers, however. When Wilson becomes involved, the name transitions to Mill Lake Development, and it is used consistently. But it's an easy detail to overlook because of previous inconsistencies.

In some ways, Foster's explanation is correct, but not in a particularly nefarious way. After the original development company was denied by the city council, Wilson simply offered the owners the most money for the land but, shrewdly, didn't officially purchase it until the development was nearly approved. After a year of digging, I finally found the document that had eluded me and confirmed this transaction: a deed of trust filed in Bonner County. In the summer of 2004, Don Wilson, along with his wife, took out a $15,000,000 loan, and with it, possession of the mill site.[8] The most reasonable explanation of how Wilson ended up with the site is that he offered Shamrock the most money for it, and they sold it to him. Months before finalizing the loan, Wilson submitted legal documents to create his new company, "Mill Lake Development," and he began presenting conceptual maps for his development at public hearings in Dover. At the first meeting in December of 2003, where three dozen people showed up, it appears that Wilson did not yet own the land. It seems he waited to sign the final paperwork until the development was only a month away from its final approval. But he does appear to then have bought the land outright.

Another popular explanation for the city council's decision to approve Wilson's development was that Wilson had bribed them. One resident told me, "Don kind of thought he could bribe them . . . and get away with anything he wanted." When I pressed residents who offered this theory for more details, most suggested that offering to build a city hall was the bribe. I would imagine that from Wilson's position it might seem like no good deed goes unpunished, and I hesitate to see something that benefits the entire community as a bribe. But even residents who supported the development and believed it turned out to be a boon for the community still offered this as an explanation. As another resident put it, after the city council said no to the idea of development, "Don waved a bunch of money, a bunch of money," and then the council approved it.

One of the people involved in the land development, a friend of Wilson's, offered a similar explanation, but one that reads much differently. "Don was really looking at how to make this an integral part of the community and not make it exclusive," he said. For him, Wilson worked hard to give back to all of Dover, with the city hall, with miles of trails, and with other amenities that he thought would sweeten the deal for existing residents.

Rumors surrounding Wilson, however, circulated freely. During multiple interviews, opponents of the development reported that Wilson had stopped them when they walked through the mill site and told them he'd have them arrested for trespassing. It seemed that everywhere I went, someone wanted to tell me a story about an interaction they (or their brother, or their ex-husband, or their coworker, or their neighbor) had had with Wilson over the years.

My own experiences of collecting data for this book highlighted Wilson's presence in the community. For example, early on in the process, I ended up at a photocopy shop in nearby Sandpoint, making copies of documents that residents had let me borrow. As I carefully tracked how many copies I was making (because in a small town like Sandpoint, you're on the honor system), a woman came up and looked at my stacks of papers. In a brusque tone, she asked me why I had "all these papers." I briefly explained that I was a college professor writing a book about Dover, and she responded, "Well, I hope Don Wilson knows what you're up to" and then turned and left. It struck me as odd that even with just a pile of old newspaper articles, she would invoke his name.

Then, when I attempted to retrieve the archaeological site report from the Army Corps of Engineers, I was told that normally these reports were released to university researchers but that this particular site report had a note on it saying that the developer liked to sue people, so they would not release it to me. I had to get my university's lawyer involved and submit a Freedom of Information Act request to get a copy. Once I reviewed the record, I realized it contained almost nothing of interest and surely nothing that wasn't to be expected. So why had it been protected so fiercely?

These stories certainly made me wonder why the only documents that seemed to be missing from the city related to three of the most important dates in Dover's timeline. Why were all the tapes in a box marked "Mill Lake Development" blank? When the tapes were stored, I was told, they worked just fine. It is hard to look at these holes and not conclude that someone was trying to hide something. But there are, for sure, more mundane explanations. One resident offhandedly described the record-keeping in Dover in the early years, saying that the notes were probably "written in lead and tree-skin bark." And many folks who had been on the city council remembered that the notes had long been stored in Mayor Jones's barn, since the city had no formal place for meetings or storage until Wilson built the new city hall as part of the development. When the boxes of notes and tapes from the city's early years had finally been moved to a storage unit attached to the public beach's restroom, they were full of mouse poop and other debris.

Even residents in the new Mill Lake development shared stories about Wilson's unusual tactics. One woman claimed that when the new high-way bypass was being built in nearby Sandpoint, Wilson thought that it was infringing on property that he owned. She claimed that the state police had to be brought in with dogs in tow to get Wilson to leave the site after he confronted the engineers. This resident said that Wilson is "the kind of person who acts first and then gets away with it nine outta ten times."

Another example of Wilson's behavior from the new Mill Lake residents concerned the hot tub in the health club at the new development. According to one, Wilson was sued by the local power company for building the hot tub under existing power lines. He had built it where he wanted it and waited for them to sue him before he agreed to move it. "The hot tub incident" was one of several small victories against Wilson, which also included requiring him to rebuild the top floor of his real estate office after residents complained that it was taller than allowed by the city code.

In all my research, I have found no evidence that Wilson is anything more than a shrewd negotiator who has an uncanny ability to invest in the right properties at the right time and who has partnered with a lawyer who rarely loses—a lawyer who attended nearly every meeting Wilson spoke at while working to develop the mill site. His lawyer has represented him since at least 1986, as far back as Bonner County's online

4.1. The Mill Lake real estate office—the upper portion of which had to be rebuilt after neighbors complained that it violated the height ordinance—ushers people into Mill Lake. In the foreground, a sign points people to the Dover Community Church.

records go. As residents were quick to point out, the first beach house built in the development—on a double lot, no less—was for Wilson's lawyer. On paper, Wilson's strategy seems to be that the best defense is a good offense. Everything I found suggested that Wilson followed the letter, though perhaps not always the spirit, of the law.

Of course, the ability of those with money and lawyers to deftly navigate the letter of the law demonstrates the structural conditions working against those opposing the development. Wilson's ability to navigate these structures—which privilege landowners and developers over the community and the environment—would be a source of anger for those interested in preserving old Dover and the local environment.

One of Wilson's ways of navigating these structures of privilege, his handling of protected wetlands, infuriated his opponents and showed how deftly he circumnavigated some environmental and archaeological regulations. Opponents insisted that the mill site was a wetland and should be protected. Since the Army Corps of Engineers has strict limits about how much land can be filled in in wetlands, they believed they could leverage this bureaucracy to slow or stop Wilson, arguing that Wilson planned to destroy large swaths of wetland. However, according to the professional wetland scientist who surveyed the land, Wilson "stayed under the limit which required mitigation."

How he stayed under this limit is controversial. Once Wilson learned that his plans to fill in large amounts of wetlands on the site would require a complex set of permits and a public hearing process, he pulled his permit with the Army Corps of Engineers. As the wetland scientist explained, Wilson's original plan "would have required actually quite a bit of work on his part: archaeological studies, biological assessments, just a whole slew of stuff." The scientist continued, "He went back and forth, arguing with the Corps . . . and ultimately came down to filling less than one-tenth of an acre, I believe." That amount kept Wilson from having to participate in a lengthier permitting process with the Army Corps of Engineering.

However, clearly, more than one-tenth of an acre of wetlands had been filled in to build the development. According to the wetlands scientist, Mill Lake Development received a new low-impact permit that allowed the filling of one-tenth of an acre of wetlands—but the permit is worded in a way that allows every single landowner, who are technically separate entities from Mill Lake Development, to fill in their tenth of an acre too.

"This does not belong to Don Wilson Incorporated, or . . . [Mill Lake] Estates, or whatever it's called," the scientist continued. "This now belongs to Joe, then Joe can fill a tenth, and Sam can fill a tenth, Mary can fill a tenth, because they're separate properties." Some of the lots are quite small, but in those cases, the new landowners could fill in a whole lot of wetlands and still operate within the terms of the permit, the scientist confirmed.

Even today, one of the opponents of the development can list off what she believes is evidence that Wilson behaved illegally when it came to the wetlands permit. In our interview, she pointed to a map of the development where the road wraps close to the old beach. "This road," she says, "isn't even permitted, because if you drive out there, you'll see a culvert going underneath. There are two fingers of the wetland, and you cannot build over that. They never got this permitted that I know of."

Other opponents point to the unintended consequences of filling in so much of the wetlands on other people's private property. What was once a dry field that used to be used as a horse pasture near the development is now flooded, perhaps due to the filling in of wetlands. The owner of that piece of land lost the use of it, conceivably due to the new development.

I asked the wetland scientist about this particular case, and he confirmed that "it's very possible" that the cumulative effect of filling wetlands on individual plots on the development could flood a property upstream. In effect, this then *creates* a wetland on a new property, which the landowner would need a permit to fill in should it get larger than one-tenth of an acre. The scientist noted that bigger development projects would bring in several agencies and require public hearings, but the cumulative effect of numerous small fills goes unregulated in Idaho and leaves residents to deal with the consequences with no regulatory support.

In this way, opponents were right to be concerned about the impact of filling the wetlands, but they found themselves squaring off against a developer who could afford the kind of legal and technical experts that allowed him to follow the letter of the law while achieving the same results. Moreover, they found that the systems of environmental regulations are not intrinsically suited to protect the environmental concerns of the community. Residents who were opposed to the development attempted to use state and federal agencies to slow the process, but like the generation of Doverites who had fought to keep the beach open (discussed in the next chapter), they found themselves in the midst of a system that made no concessions for the rights of communities against landowners with a lawyer.

Amid this situation, opponents generally directed their frustrations at the actors rather than the system itself. Longtime residents who had fought to keep the beach public for decades and had run out of avenues to preserve their most beloved spaces had in many ways come to understand that they had no systemic protections, so they hung their hopes on the "local boy" developer. These residents of old Dover supported the development in many cases out of a sense that it was inevitable, but they hoped to leverage their personal connections to preserve the community's access and connection to the site. In particular, they were satisfied with the understanding that they would have perpetual access to the docks, from which they could fish and launch their fishing boats. Those stipulations never made it into writing, however, and without any tapes of the meetings, it is the word of the community against a paper trail that was not concerned with these details.

Of course, while many people in the community were happy to rail at length about Wilson's tactics, others spoke warmly about him. A planner for the development claimed that Wilson was not simply looking out for his own profits.

As the scientists above noted, however, once the developer agreed to fill in less than a tenth of an acre, he could determine which land—likely the wetland with the culvert—should be filled and the permit the opponent mentioned was no longer a concern. When pressed about what the motivation to develop might be, if not money, he argued that "in the little cabins right here when you're next to city hall, there's a monument to the developer's father. . . . His children are involved, his wife's involved. He wants to leave a legacy."

This perspective, however, was largely not shared by the Dover community. For most of Dover, Wilson's tactics and his personality became lightning rods for the development process, drawing out residents' anger, frustration, and sadness. The larger history of Dover and rural communities in the American West, however, suggests that Wilson was simply working within the boundaries of a system that put his interests and those of other landowners above the desires of community members and certainly above environmental concerns.

CONCLUSION

By framing the process of development as the result of a bad actor or a consequence of unresponsive and underresourced bureaucracies, the larger system of inequality and exploitation remains invisible. In my hours and hours of interviewing, there was almost no discussion of the larger economic context that Dover exists within. For most residents who opposed the development, they saw themselves as simply outlawyered by a shrewd developer.

The people who opposed the Mill Lake development lost faith in the political or legal systems' ability to protect their interests. Just as with the old-timers, who had already learned that the legal system wouldn't protect community interests, a sense of hopelessness spread to those who opposed the development and were left gutted by the process. One said they'd quit participating in local issues. Others simply left the community they loved for good.

The old-timers blame Californian migrants for the negative changes in their community and often waxed poetic about how good the mill owners in the 1960 and 1970s had been, how wonderful their lives had been. The opposition to the development blamed Don Wilson for exploiting the community, something that they now have in common with the old-timers. But these narratives are all deeply ahistorical. It is vastly easier to blame some person or group of people for one's loss of power. It is much harder to acknowledge that the very system in which you have built your community isn't designed to allow them to exercise power. And in the rural West, is it next to impossible to articulate how you fit into a long history of exploitation that never intended to build sustainable communities for ordinary people in the first place.

5

Anarchists on the Beach

AMY BROWN WAS raised in Dover surrounded her by grandparents, aunts, uncles, and cousins. Her ex-husband worked for the mill, and together they raised their children in Dover. A few days a week, her grandson comes over after school and catches snakes in her yard, just as she had done in her youth and then her own children did. For years, she volunteered for the city, but despite (or perhaps because of) her deep ties in the community, she decided early on not to become invested in the debates surrounding the development. She found it emotionally overwhelming.

"Oh, I was scared," she remembered. "I am . . . the type of person that figures: why worry about something that hasn't happened? I finally had to do that. Otherwise, I was going to have a nervous breakdown."

Like Brown, many of Dover's longtime residents who had been born and raised there attended the city council meetings as the plan to build a six-hundred-unit, upscale development on the old mill site was debated. However, they rarely spoke at those meetings, choosing instead to sit on the sidelines watching. Ted Foster, a resident who had worked to stop the development, believed that their reluctance was due to the "local boy" developer, who led some residents to be "very reserved or shy about standing up and saying anything in front of [him]." The records suggest that many of the older residents seemed, if not enthusiastic about the change, at least resigned to it.

So, while many Dover residents were mounting a campaign against the development (as discussed in the previous chapter), other residents quietly opted out of the debate. This schism was largely defined by age and the length of their ties to Dover. The residents who actively resisted the development were younger and were often themselves considered outsiders, since they had not been born and raised in the area. In Dover, thirty years of residency still makes you a "newcomer," according to those whose families were some of the original settlers or who arrived on horse-pulled wagons as Dust Bowl refugees in the 1930s, settling into houses abandoned during the Great Depression. These longtime residents largely accepted that a new development was going to happen, though sometimes begrudgingly so.

The failure of these different groups to come together against the development at first glance defies logic. For both groups, everything that was worth preserving in Dover was symbolized by one vital space: the city's sandy beach and the rocky bluff overlooking it. Dover's beach had long been a beloved place in the community, serving for generations as a swimming hole, picnic spot, baptismal font, gathering place, and hiking area. The area was also a wetland that cleansed the water, and the bluff provided a habitat for the native camas, a tall purple flower whose roots were a staple for the Kalispel people. Saving the beach and bluff was tantamount to saving the idea of Dover itself for almost all of the residents facing the prospect of the development.

Both groups understood the significance of the bluff and the beach to the people of Dover, but they struggled to articulate a shared vision of the importance of those spaces. The residents who mounted a campaign against the development framed their arguments in environmental and ecological terms, creating a narrative around the beach and bluff that did not align with the vision of the old-timers. Arguments for preserving the wetlands were also out of tune with the old-timers, who were generally not ideologically supportive of environmentalism as a movement and who were far more concerned with a nostalgic sense of community leisure time. Old-timers did not see a possible environmental disaster. With a sense of resignation, they saw an idyllic past of community and camaraderie that had already been eroded over the years by economic decline and callous landowners. For the old-timers, the beach and the bluff were spaces of community merrymaking—places to fish, to have bonfires, to teach your children to swim. If the development could bring more young folks back to the community, perhaps a small part of that past could be reclaimed, and maybe sacrificing the beach would be worth it.

In this way, the schisms between residents of old Dover mirror the long-standing and politically fraught debates that have been framed as between environmentalism and the economic needs of rural communities. These debates exploded into a national media spectacle in the early 1990s as loggers vented their frustration with new environmental rules protecting the habitat of the spotted owl. But the idea that environmental regulations were intrinsically opposed to job creation and community well-being in rural spaces had been building throughout the 1980s, and they have become entrenched in contemporary US politics around the country, not just in the West.[1]

This cultural-political divide helped ensure that opposition to the Mill Lake development never coalesced beyond a small but vocal group of Dover residents who thought that environmental regulations might protect the community's beloved beach and bluff. That rhetoric failed to win over the much older Dover residents who prioritized the possibility of new jobs and a rejuvenated community over the habitat of the camas flower.

However, the reticence of the old-timers was more nuanced than simple knee-jerk opposition to environmentalism as a movement. After all, decades earlier, those same residents had mounted an active campaign to protect and preserve the beach for the community. The old-timers had learned then that the rights of the community were never going to surmount the legal rights of private property owners. Frustrated and worn down by their own powerlessness, it seemed unlikely to them that bureaucratic environmental regulations would somehow protect the rights of the community to enjoy the beach.

What is clear based on the histories discussed in previous chapters is that rural timber communities were built according to an ideology that put the interests of the wealthy over those of the workers. This was coupled with the rural West's ideology of "rugged individualism," which posits that individual rights supersede those of the collective. These ideological forces maintain the political systems that disempower local communities, particularly in Idaho.

In the preceding chapter, I suggested that creating a space for capitalism is about building an ideological and structural system to support it, all while working to make that system seem inevitable and natural. Similarly, the process of "destroying" a space to make way for new forms of economic exploitation is not just about a building burning down or eliminating jobs but instead about the "decay of social infrastructures and loss of communal solidarities."[2]

Ultimately in Dover, the community failed to create an effective resistance to the development not only because of lost wages and population decline but because Dover's sense of itself as a community was disrupted after the closure of the mill. The town became more fragmented and was unable to mount a unified resistance to the development. By exploring the beach and the various efforts to save it, this chapter explores these failures and the subsequent demoralization of Dover, the fallout of which remains today.

THE UNCANNY QUIET

Lindsey Green was one of the "newcomers" who moved to Dover after her divorce because she could afford a rundown double-wide there in the late 1990s. But she had lived in the area for twenty years before that and had been visiting Dover for decades. Like so many others, the bluff was a special place for her. She lovingly remembered her first date with her former husband there. Over a picnic of peanut butter–and-jelly sandwiches on white bread, they fished and wondered at the natural beauty of the rocks that made up the bluff. She had visited it and the beach over the decades, and she loved how "the rocks up there in the spring are completely covered with camas root. You sit in the moss up there and you can look out. . . . Then there's wildflowers all spring, and the first ones that come up are the camas root. I spent a lot of time just there, a lot. I love just sitting there."

Green's love for the beach and the bluff in Dover led her to fight the development. She was one of the many people who wrote articles and editorials for the local papers, trying to convince the broader community of the essential ecological and cultural roles these natural spaces of Dover played (as described in the previous chapter). And she was not alone. As the Dover old-timers sat on the sidelines, the efforts to halt the development fell primarily to the newer residents of old Dover, like Green. These were teachers and bookkeepers, artists and farmers. They actively opposed the development and were tireless in their efforts to stop it.

Their efforts specifically relied on an ideological framework of environmentalism and conservation. They argued that the development would be harmful to the environment, the wetlands in particular. As I described in chapter 4, many opponents thought that government regulations concerning wetland protection would provide the best legal leverage to stop or slow down the development, not knowing how deftly the developer would be able to skirt such regulations. This ecological frame shows up in every public hearing comment, every letter to the editor, and every interview.

"They didn't listen to any of us," Lee Bell told me when discussing the environmental impact of the development. "My biggest concern is simply the fact that they built on a wetland." Bell, like others, opposed the development and attempted to convince neighbors that it would be devastating to the wetlands. In a letter to the editor, another opponent of the development implored, "This land teems with wildlife and wildflowers and offers a much-needed green space in an ever more crowded river valley."[3]

Another Dover resident wrote, "The land's highest and best use for this property is not development, but environment." For this resident, the wetlands were home to birds and wildlife and cleansed the river, keeping it "navigable and useful to man and beast."[4] For their efforts, one opponent remembers thinking that the old-timers "just thought I was a big pothead."

More specifically, the old-timers did not look around at old Dover and see a pristine wilderness they were desperate to preserve. In fact, after years of neglect and decay, they did not see much worth preserving at all. They had spent the last several decades watching their community slowly wither after the closure of the mill, ushering in an unfamiliar period of sadness and stillness. "For a while, it was kind of uncanny," Amy Brown remembered of that period after the mill closed. "It was scary, I guess because it was so quiet. It was really, super quiet, and we were always used to hearing the machinery running and everything. That was comforting. Then, all of a sudden, we didn't hear that. Everybody was out of work and everything."

Some residents were therefore optimistic that the development might help remake Dover into the kind of community they remembered from decades earlier. They hoped that the hustle and bustle of the new development would shatter the uncanny silence of the old community. Of course, they understood that it would be very different from the Dover they remembered, but they hoped it would put the city back on the map.

Some old-timers also found it difficult to see the supposedly pristine natural environment described by the opponents. The opponents tried to convince their neighbors that the development would forever alter the ecology of the site, but for many residents who had grown up with the mill running, they saw it as intrinsically blighted. They believed that the piles of sawdust that were left behind were eyesores and health hazards.

Sarah Walker, who had grown up in Dover, said, "I remember the smell of the mill more than I remember what it looked like, and it's so different out there now." She remembered how, after the rain, the smell of wet sawdust would "permeate Dover." Fred Young also remembered the sawdust, suggesting that the well-manicured development with walking paths is much preferable to the sawdust that was left behind at the mill site. "It's much nicer than just having big sawdust piles there and nothing [else]," he said.

The health concerns surrounding those piles of sawdust were also on the minds of the old-timers. "Well, number one, you wonder about the number of people who've had respiratory issues and everything because of the mill," Amy Brown said, remembering how the wind pushed the sawdust particles into the town. "It blew constantly. You know you had to be breathing that."

John White put the environmental blight of the old mill in even starker terms, suggesting that, in addition to the sawdust piles, the mill site experienced years of chemical contamination. According to White, in the 1960s, when the mill was a Tenax plant using wood chips to produce particleboard, the mill employees disposed of their industrial waste on-site. "When those fifty-five-gallon drums of that glue would go bad," he claimed, "they would dump [them] out there. They would dump that chemical out there. If you look where that dog park walkway is, you can still see it bubbling up out of the ground. How they can even build there on contaminated waste, I'll never know."

When he raised these concerns with the developer's son over drinks at the local bar one evening, White claims that the developer's son told him to "shut the fuck up . . . People don't want to hear that." But White insists that the story of the dumping, as told to him by his father, is true.

Evan Johnson also claimed that the new development is more ecologically sound than the old mill site. For Johnson, "the old mill site was pretty much a mess. You get used to a mess. You don't really see all the old cables and stuff sticking up and the old, rotting railroad ties and the creosote and the dirt and the old oil that they used to dump. You just never really saw it if you went by it."

Like many of the old-timer residents, Johnson was happy with the finished project of the development. "Actually, I think it's a major improvement, ecologically and visually, [over] what it used to be," he said.

In this way, the older-timers and those who fought the development based on environmental terms seemed to see old Dover in very different terms. Opponents to the development saw a peaceful, rural community with an idyllic ecology worth protecting. But many old-timer residents looked around and saw an environmental blight left behind by the timber economy that had painfully abandoned them. Opponents of the development touted the important ecological role of the wetlands, but old-timers felt that poured walkways and well-maintained lawns might be preferable to the sawdust piles and chemical contamination that they associated with the mill site. The ecological arguments of the opponents, in short, were just not compelling for the old-timers, who had some ecological concerns of their own.

Moreover, old-timer residents grieved the loss of the Dover of their youth and remained nostalgic for the years they had spent growing up and raising their children there. They hoped the development would potentially offer an approximation of that lost sense of community. The land planner for the development noted as much when saying, "With the mill closing down, which had been for some time, they [the old-timers] were really very supportive, to try to get more vitality back within Dover."

5.1. The new beach on the river that the developer donated to the people of Dover. The riprap and gravel the old-timers disliked are visible.

they saw as fundamentally unfair attempts to keep people from accessing what they believed to be a public beach but was, legally speaking, private property. They had, over the past several decades, agitated enthusiastically against what they felt were unethical laws governing the community's rights to access the beach. An alliance with newer residents who wanted to stop a development that would eliminate all access to the beach and bluff would seem to have been logical. But by the time the development came around, these old-timers were worn out from decades of systematic attempts by various property owners to force Dover residents to give up their claims to the beach, and they did not feel as though they had much fight left in them.

At first glance, it seems there certainly could have been an opportunity for the two sides to come together to preserve these spaces for the public. Sharon Miller had arrived in Dover as a young girl, her family leaving behind the devastation of the 1930s Dust Bowl. In the midst of her living room, lovingly decorated with paintings of elk and other wildlife, stands a photo of her as a child with her siblings and cousins in front of the wagon in which they had traveled hundreds and hundreds of miles. Sharon served as a sort of community spokesperson, because she said exactly what she was thinking. And she was unequivocal about her feelings about watching her much-beloved beach and bluff cut off from the people of Dover.

I had not even officially started the interview when Sharon said, "What [they] did, [they] took advantage of us. Sold that bluff. If we had it to do again, we would have never let him have the bluff or the swimming hole. Never! Because that is worth a million of the lot. [Mill Lake Development] did take advantage of the Dover people, I will say that." While the opposition felt that old-timers were intimidated by the developer, in my interviews they often spoke quite openly and negatively about him. If they were intimidated in 2004, they were not by 2017. It seems their silence may have been an attempt to build an alliance with him, because they realized they had very few legal avenues to maintain access to public spaces.

Given Miller's strong objections to the closing off of these "commons," it might seem surprising that the old-timers and those fighting the development could not find a way to come together to at least preserve the beach and the bluff for public enjoyment. But the record suggests that this effort likely did not materialize because the old-timers, even Sharon Miller, believed they had already lost the fight for the beach. Starting in the 1970s, locals had agitated against the mill owners for access to the beach. And continuing in the late 1990s, the development group that owned the mill site, Shamrock (aka Dover Development), again spent significant energy on restricting public access. It seems likely this was an effort to test the community's power to fight for this valuable land.

As John White, a middle-aged man who had generations of family in Dover, noted, the beach in Dover was "the last of the sand beaches." He gestured to the imagined banks of the river and lake, and said the rest of it is "all mud-bottom slop." For the developer, this single, sandy-beached, lakefront lot alone was likely worth nearly 10 percent of the loan he'd taken out to fund the development. Any potential buyer would have been very much interested in understanding what rights the locals had to that particular piece of land. The people of Dover loved the beach and were not afraid to fight for it—and they had been for the last thirty years—but lacked any legal rights to it. In fact, White said that he had gone door-to-door with Mayor Jones's daughter, gathering signatures for a petition to keep the beach open when they were teenagers.

Many of the old-timers recalled that the first beach closures happened in July of 1978, when the then-owners, the Pack River Lumber Company, closed the road leading to the beach, the bluff, and the baseball field because of "theft, vandalism, fire, sanitation, and no lifeguard." Residents were undeterred: "I've been walking that beach for forty years, and I'm not about to stop now," one woman defiantly told a newspaper reporter.[7] Residents took different approaches to keep the space open to the public.

They organized, filing petitions, writing letters, and involving local government. The letter-writers all took a similar approach, arguing that the residents of Dover had been accessing that space for fifty years and that it was public property. In a long letter to the editor, one resident carefully dismantled the lumber company's assertion that beach was being closed due to "theft, vandalism, fire, sanitation, and no lifeguard," though the author does evocatively grant that, "sanitation—well, I'll have to concede that point—it could be improved." But then the 1978 letter goes on to presciently ask, "Can you tell me why, after all these years, it has finally become such a major conflict? Has Pack River decided to close down the beach in order to build some condominiums there now? I suspect an ulterior motive is in the offing. That's just about all the quiet, peaceful community of Dover needs now. A great big new housing development."[8]

Residents also collected data about how the road to the beach was used in a handwritten table. Carefully written with four columns using a distinctive cursive are the names, addresses (nearly all post office box numbers), phone numbers (all five digits), and comments of all who used the road. This allowed whoever collected the signatures to know the "types of uses made of the road [i.e.,] to get to the beach, to get to [the] ball field, to get to the picnic area, any other use made, whether walked, biked, motorcycled, car, frequency of use over years." Covering five lined pages, the table is a time capsule of familiar names and includes the number of years each family had used the road, which in 1978 averaged thirty.[9] Most of the people on it are still in Dover forty years later. A huge photo in the *Bonner County Daily Bee* from 1978 shows no fewer than ten children standing on the beach, protest signs in hand, reading "For the Children of Dover" and "Preserve Nature's Beauty!!"

While some residents were signing petitions and others were making signs, still others were taking more direct measures to keep the beach open. When Pack River Lumber erected a dirt barricade across the road, someone plowed through it and remade the road. In response, Pack River stacked logs across the road. It was a court order that temporarily reopened the beach after thirty residents hired a lawyer and a judge put a temporary injunction in place to keep it open until the case was heard, essentially giving residents use of the beach the rest of the summer.

The lumber company and residents did not stop their public opinion campaigns, and both sides continued spilling ink in letters to the editor for the rest of that summer. In an unsigned letter on behalf of Pack River Lumber, the company tried to dispel the idea that prior use of the beach granted residents continued use. They offered a variety of examples: "If a person has access to a store, does he establish a right to that entire store without the owner's permission?" The letter concluded by offering—though not clarifying why—the "Webster's College Dictionary" definition of "ANARCHIST" (emphasis theirs).[10]

Soon the county commissioners were asked to weigh in on the decision (remember, Dover didn't become a city for nearly twenty more years). The spokesmen for the residents told the commissioners that they were willing to come up with some kind of "contractual agreement between Pack River Lumber and a nonprofit corporation of Dover residents." They also asked commissioners to look into "acquiring State Department of Parks funds or federal money to buy the beach and put in a boat launch."[11]

The residents pushed to have the county commissioners take up the case but were stalled when the county prosecutor concluded, "The county can bring suit, but it is my fear we will lose."[12] Despite his prognostication, it seems that neither side was anxious for a court battle, because by the end of 1978, a spokesman for the lumber company said that their "attitude had always been [one] of cooperation with local residents."[13]

Brown remembered that period distinctly, saying, "'78 is when they closed the beach. . . . at that time, I think they were already kind of deciding that they wanted to develop it, so they wanted to wean the Doverites off of the beach. They [the residents] just kept using it," she continued, laughing now. "Yeah, they just—they'd get upset 'cause kids would keep going down there. They'd keep driving down there. Then they put a big berm up at the end of the road. Then you had to go over the berm to go to the beach. You kept on going. They didn't mind going over a berm."

A tenuous truce emerged after the dispute in 1978, after which residents were once again given access to the beach and the road, while Pack River Lumber retained ownership of the land. For another fifteen years, young people in particular continued to skirt the berm of dirt and the "no trespassing" sign to spend their days on the beach and bluff without much resistance. But in the 1990s, soon after the land was sold to Shamrock, residents' access to the beach was more seriously restricted. Barricades, fences, and gates were erected to keep them out. In response, what was by then the City of Dover looked into ways to preserve beach access and—as was the case twenty years earlier—more than fifty residents signed a petition, likely the one White remembered circulating with Mayor Jones's daughter. In fact, it was only days after a judge ruled that Dover acted in good faith when it rezoned the mill site—and was not responsible for knowing about and informing the developer about the restrictions put in place by the USDA loan used to build the new sewer— that city officials met to begin again looking for a way to maintain public access to the beach.[14]

At the same time, the site owners were likely becoming more anxious to sell and concerned about the restrictions the USDA loan put on their development plans, as well as the city's prior threat of eminent domain to build the sewer (see chapter 3 for a full discussion). Shamrock then stepped up its efforts to keep residents off the beach. Their caretaker who lived on the site and the local teenagers became locked in an almost cartoonesque battle for beach access, including one incident in which the caretaker hit a teenager on the head with a pipe. When the pipe did not stop the swimmers and parties, the site owners dumped industrial waste—dozens of giant sections of old mill pipe—on the beach. Then barbed wire "traps" were strung under bushes to catch teens who tried to hide in them during the caretaker's patrols. The traps may or may not have been retribution for the barbed wire that the caretaker said was strung under the dirt to puncture his tires.[15]

Despite local residents' efforts, which had continued for decades, the struggles to preserve access to the beach proved futile. The city found itself stymied by the particular wording of "prescriptive easement," language that can occasionally be used by communities to claim private land that has been historically used as a public space. An Idaho Supreme Court case that emphasized individual property rights further frustrated these efforts.[16]

Old-timers like Fred and Sandy Young—who had lived in Dover for nearly eighty years and watched generations of their family learn to swim at the beach—offered another avenue of resistance for the community to maintain beach access. The Youngs were one of three families interviewed who claimed that the beach, or a path to the beach, had been given to the people of Dover by the original mill owner. "There was a paper, at one time, in the courthouse, where there's a path that went down to the beach for baptism," Fred said. "[My brother] said that there was a paper there that said that. Then they tried to find it and couldn't find it." According to these residents, the mill owner who had established Dover had been quite religious, and his brother had served as the pastor for the church. Old-time residents said that this owner—A. C. White—had gifted the people of Dover the Community Church, which still offers services on Sunday. Along with the church, according to these residents, came access to the beach, as long as the church was operating, in order to perform baptisms. Many people looked for the paperwork, believing the county had a copy, but the county seats in Idaho had been rearranged over the decades, courthouses had burned down, relatives who remembered seeing it had died, and ultimately, the trail to the paperwork went cold. But several old-time residents remembered seeing this paper supposedly granting them "access to the water for baptism." And another resident reported that she'd gone looking for the paper and "thought she was closing in on that in the documents in the court house" only to find that, in the file where it should have been, there were "pages removed from the thing."

In retrospect, some of the older residents were angry that they hadn't fought harder to retain the beach and the bluff. Mayor Jones, who had spent many years attempting to keep the beach as a public space, seemed to take its loss particularly hard. "I see things in black and white rather than in grays," he said, "and to me, that was sick and wrong. I tried everything that I could do to prevent that [the loss of the beach] from happening." But he also understood firsthand that the city simply didn't have any leverage or funds to retain the site, because they didn't legally own it.

The beach had served as a common space for the community of Dover for nearly a hundred years, but these debates about who "owns" the land are part of a much larger history of exploitation. The beach and the bluff, after all, had served as communal space for the Kalispel and other peoples for at least eight thousand years. The beach only became "property" after the US government and then the State of Idaho used military force to push the Kalispel people, along with all other Indigenous people who used this watershed, from their homeland and onto reservations. The government then gave away huge tracts of this land to corporate interests to bolster their claim to the wilderness and helped those businesses try to quash any unrest when their workers attempted to fight for their rights as laborers. Timber, mining, and railroads may have brought people to the West to form communities like Dover, but those industries were only committed to the extraction of resources, not the creation of communities.

So when Dover residents fought for the community's right to the beach, they were also fighting against a hundred years of history that rationalized a system of land ownership that never had the community's interests at heart.

CONCLUSION: THE BEACH TODAY

Today, the old sandy beach sits quiet. The lot it sits on was sold quickly after the development was okayed. For a period, a "no trespassing" sign hung across the grassy field that led from the road to the water's edge and seemed to be largely effective in keeping people's nostalgia from tempting them past the cable and into the water. Today, the home that sits there obscures the view of the lake and beach. The gift of time has led most people, opponents and old-timers alike, to agree that the development is largely well done. The miles of public trails and the city hall, in particular, have mostly won them over, but the loss of the beach and the bluff seems to have, if anything, become more painful with time. The slop-bottomed "Goose-Shit Beach" is no replacement for the old Dover beach of their youth.

Tim Casten grew up in Dover and had a way of carefully considering his words. When we talked about the old beach, he said, "I was obviously disappointed that [our beach] didn't stay where it is. You know, they moved it out. I can understand the reasoning. I mean, look at the value of that property. I can understand the developer doing that, but I will give him credit: at least he set aside an area for a Dover beach area. I appreciate that, but it's not the same. It's not the same as [the original beach] and having our little nighttime bonfires there and getting up on the bluff and jumping into the water and all those kinds of things."

One of the men who played a key role in the development, Ben Smith was sympathetic to a point, as he acknowledged: "There will be change. There will be change, without a doubt. It's very, very difficult. I think more difficult in this neck of the woods, from my experience in other areas. Just because you do have folks that've been residents for eighty years. That's the way it's been. We really tried to look at [the old beach] as a potential for the beach, but . . . they also have a beach. It's not like it was taken away." He points to a map where the new beach sits. "It was just transferred for a better opportunity. Here you've got estuary and inlet bays and also riverfront, the same that you didn't have before."

The people of Dover had been working to preserve their access to the beach for decades before it became part of Mill Lake Development's holdings, and there was little doubt that the bluff and sandy beach were the most economically valuable places. They were ripe for development. Smith noted as much, saying, "[The original beach] was really the public beach at that time. That had to be—that's also a prime development site. Parks were put together, and a new city hall, and recreation center. There are a lot of great amenities." And he pushed back against some of the frustrations about the loss when discussing the residents: "Well, I just think that a lot of people don't know what goes into a development. Believe me, it's not greed-driven. Payback on this particular property takes a long, long time. Yes, there are developers that'll be down and dirty, and believe me, I've worked for them. This particular developer is not that breed. He's too connected to the fabric here."

But some of the old-timers felt different. Sharon Miller said it plainly: "I don't care. If I ever seen [the owner of the development], I'd say, 'You did a sin.'" That frustration is largely born of what feels like a double standard. As one resident poetically said, "There was a freedom which is gone now. It's all heavily regulated. Regulated by people who don't want to comply with regulations."

Remember, the people of Dover were without drinkable water for six years because they could not legally compel the owners of the mill site to continue to provide drinkable water. Yet they were forced to rezone the land in the developer's favor after the developers refused to sell them the land to build a sewer and then took them to court to force a sort of quid pro quo. After that, the people of Dover did the work of funding and planning the water and sewer infrastructure. Then Shamrock turned around and sold the land at a huge profit, precisely because it was set up for municipal water and sewer service. This was all happening as Shamrock paid a caretaker who hit teens on the head with pipes and was reportedly setting barbed wire traps to keep them off the beach.

As was discussed in more detail in the preceding chapter, opponents of the Mill Lake development desperately tried to use laws and regulatory systems to stop it. They involved the Army Corps of Engineers to stop the wetlands from being filled in. As a result, the developer only filled in a tenth of an acre but carefully worded the permit so every single unit in the development could also fill in a tenth of an acre. Opponents called Idaho Fish and Game when they believed a tree with a bald eagle's nest was being cut down to build a road, but they were told by a sympathetic game warden that the agency didn't have anyone who could get there in time. In short, they found out, painfully, that being right wasn't sufficient. The system was not set up for them to ever really win.

The old-timers learned that lesson over and over in the previous decades, and by the time the final developer arrived with plans, they lacked faith in the system, even those who worked in the system, to protect their interests in the community. Instead, they put whatever little faith they had left in the strength of their history and relationships. They hoped that the "local boy" developer would do right by them, not exactly because they trusted him but because they had so little trust in the system to protect them.

Ironically, both those who opposed the development and the old-timers who didn't were struggling with the same frustration: the system of laws in place didn't protect them or their community rights, only the rights of property owners. Old-timers struggled to find any legal grounds to protect community access to the beach, because property laws are not structured to truly consider the needs of communities, only individuals, while opponents of the development found that appeals based on environmental laws and regulations elicited little enforcement that actually protected the community.

6

A Mill Lake Moment

YOU CANNOT GET to Dover without driving. Come from the south—as most people do—and you'll see the last hundred years of history in the region in the towns and the landscape. You will follow the rail lines and likely see train after a train loaded with oil tankers from the Bakken oil fields in North Dakota on their way to Washington. These trains are reminders that a new extractive industry is king in other, less scenic parts of the American West. You will also pass through towns like Careywood, Westmond, and Sagle. Before the highway was widened, you would have had to slow down a bit, but now you can zip through most of them at seventy miles an hour. Then, without any warning, the forest will open, and you will hit the Long Bridge into Sandpoint. Locals complain that you can't get anyone to drive even as fast as the fifty-five-mile-an-hour speed limit on the bridge—they're too busy taking in the view. Mountains ring the lake, with Schweitzer Mountain Ski Resort ahead of you, and you're almost guaranteed to see a bald eagle perched on one of the cottonwoods toward the north end.

This short drive reveals the three fates of the American West as geographer Joe Weber sees it: destined to be either booming, bypassed, or protected.[1] The Careywoods and Westmonds, for example, represent the bypassed West. Unless you need a quick tank of gas or maybe want to try your luck at "the Careywood mall" (the dump)—which among a certain demographic in North Idaho functions as a low-key thrift store—you're not likely to notice that the assemblage of buildings on the side of the road even constitutes a town. Maybe they were once stops along the train line or key respites when people traveled by horse, but today they seem mostly to be an inconvenience for travelers anxious to make it to the lake or ski mountain. The population of these towns is dwindling. Their best hope is that locals get priced out of communities like Sandpoint (and now Dover) and will move farther south, away from the shores of the lake and the tourists.

The region includes the protected West too. Around Sagle, you'll pass Round Lake State Park, where I spent a fateful summer scrubbing down campground bathrooms and befriending an eyeless wiener dog. The park is a space set aside for the public good and mostly nonextractive purposes. You can camp, fish, and hike (or ski) around the small lake. The protected West also includes the numerous national forests, recreation areas, and wildlife preserves in the vicinity.

The protection of these spaces for recreation has helped fuel a boom in some parts of the American West, such as Sandpoint, where the scenic beauty has drawn new populations of "amenity migrants." As towns in the West that relied on extractive industries to fuel their economy began to struggle, some reinvented themselves to accommodate newcomers and part-timers with the money to ski, boat, and recreate in the rustic beauty that makes the American West what people imagine it to be. Of course, as the oil trains rumbling through every hour attest, other kinds of western towns are booming as well, this time organized around other extractive industries.

The wholesale shift of Dover from a mill town to a self-described "planned residential, waterfront resort community" moved it nearly over-night from bypassed to booming. Unlike Careywood or Westmond, Dover's position on the water, where Lake Pend Oreille meanders into the Pend Oreille River, dramatically altered the town's trajectory in the history of the West. Labor to process timber products might not be val-ued anymore, but Dover had a new commodity to be extracted and pack-aged for consumers: beauty and wilderness.

This chapter explores the transformations that have taken place in Dover and how those changes reflect the shifting meanings of the rural

West. In particular, I examine here how the spaces of Dover have changed: how the new development restructured the community and the residents' relationship to the natural world. The Mill Lake development represented more than new buildings and more people: it offered a fundamentally different way of relating to space and nature than found in the lifeways of old Dover. While the latter had long been characterized by a casual use of "common" (but privately owned) spaces that brought the community together, Mill Lake sought to commodify and tightly manage access to beaches, the water, and the wild for residents both old and new.

The two Dovers that emerged in the wake of the development, then, did not just look different, they represented vastly different assumptions about the uses and meaning of space and the environment, assumptions fundamentally rooted in social class distinctions. Of course, this is to be expected under the logic of the spatial fix, where capitalism first creates landscapes and then later destroys them when they are not profitable, setting the stage for "openings for fresh accumulation in new spaces and territories."[2] Applying this concept to the development, we can see how the construction of Mill Lake literally built a new space that could be organized for consumption rather than labor, but was nevertheless designed for profit.

Needless to say, building communities around profit rather than the organic needs of the people in those communities makes it difficult to build solidarity between people of different backgrounds. The new development and its vision of space and nature spurred divisions between the two communities (old Dover and the development) rather than bringing people from diverse backgrounds together. After all, the new development was designed to privilege class-based visions of recreation, bodies, and environmentalism, visions that often exclude the people of what is sometimes now called "old Dover."

CHANGE IN THE AMERICAN WEST

There are almost no communities in Idaho that look the way they did a generation ago. Instead, there are two paths that most communities have followed: rapid population loss or rapid population growth. The development in Dover is an almost perfect case study of growth in rural communities since the mid-1980s. As the jobs from extractive industries disappeared, some communities were reinvented, as long as they had the scenery and amenities that appealed to those who could afford to become permanent tourists. Since the 1980s, communities with "high levels of natural amenities," such as Dover, have been transformed by "amenity-driven rural population growth."[3]

To describe these processes, scholars have developed various taxonomies for understanding the change wrought by "amenity migration," or "the purchasing of primary or second residences in rural areas valued for their aesthetic, recreational, and other consumption-orientated use-values."[4] For example, Richelle Winkler et al., alongside other scholars, see the population increases from amenity migration as a key factor in the creation of a kind of "New West."[5] Juxtaposed against the cultural fantasy of the "Old West"—conjuring images of "ranchers, horses, and dusty cattle drives"—the so-called New West represents a new set of social structures and cultural identities for rural towns.[6] Evoking images of "residents wearing Patagonia fleeces" instead of traditional Western wear, the denizens of this New West are often thought of as professionals working remotely on their laptops or else "retirees seeking a lifestyle tied to the natural environment and the slower pace of country living, as well as growing numbers of seasonal residents who divide their time between city and country."[7] For towns with the scenic and recreational amenities to offer newcomers, population growth has become the norm, but this has not simply meant new economic arrangements and employment opportunities. It has yielded new forms of cultural identities and altered social structures for rural communities.

The story of the New West became familiar in many parts of Idaho as the towns that had supported extractive industries tried to save themselves through tourist dollars, and not just in former timber communities. In the Silver Valley, a few hours southeast of Dover, most of the mining is now done by machines, and the communities there are trying to rebrand as historic mountain villages. In Wallace, Idaho, you can learn about the history of mining in local museums and attractions that take tourists into old mine tunnels. The jobs that once made Wallace one of the most important cities in the state are now a source of nostalgia for tourists on their way to the nearby ski slopes. The streets are lined with antique stores and restaurants catering to the influx of tourists in the region. Of course, as in many former mining towns turned tourist stops, visitors are cautioned not to swim or eat the fish from the water because of the toxic mine tailings.

Winkler et al. are careful to note that the emergence of the New West is not a uniform transition across the American West but rather an uneven set of economic, social, and cultural changes impacting some communities while others continue to struggle. In this way, Weber's taxonomy of the "booming, bypassed, and protected" Wests offers an alternative characterization of the Old versus New West. As I noted above, Weber sees the changes in the American West as multifaceted, with some communities experiencing the "booms" of tourism and population growth, some areas experiencing job loss and population decline, and other areas having been set aside as national or state parks, wilderness areas, or wildlife refuges that often serve as playgrounds for the populations of the booming West.[8]

The fates of these different Wests, then, are intertwined. Booming areas mean that others will necessarily be bypassed, creating a series of winners and losers based on the natural beauty and amenities that some regions can offer, although the bypassed West will still be used for spaces to accommodate new growth and new booms. Access to the wilderness in the form of protected lands, likewise, often supports booming communities by providing scenic beauty and recreational activities, but government-protected lands also provide limitations to growth by ensuring that some aren't subject to development and population expansion. The booming West might align neatly with the idea of the New West, but the latter has only emerged as part of the complex geography of change in the West.

Additionally, some booming communities in the West are not aligned with the cultural identity of the New West, having emerged in the wake of new forms of extractive industries. For example, a combination of technological innovation and increased gas prices meant that almost overnight, rigs were built outside sleepy towns in Montana and North Dakota in the 2000s to extract oil from the deposits below the surface. Formerly quiet towns such as Williston, North Dakota, became boomtowns, where working-class men from around the country sought their fortune, swelling the populations of these tiny communities and straining their resources. So many men from small towns in Idaho left for the oil fields that they called their encampments things like "Little Salmon," an homage to the towns they left behind. Like the boomtowns of the early twentieth century, the oil fields were plagued with extreme housing shortages and a surge of violent crime, particularly against women. The booming West of the Bakken oil fields, however, was atypical, particularly in the rural West.

Regardless of the taxonomy used to characterize the changes that have transformed the American West over the past several decades, this transition has been marked by very different visions of space and the utility of nature, as new ways of commodifying the wilderness have yielded new kinds of communities. The Old West is imagined (fairly or not) as embodying a man-versus-nature relationship, where, in places like Dover, men with chainsaws and skidders tamed the woods. This gendered vision of the landscape and its uses is oversimplified, but it captures some of the core assumptions around the utility of nature in Old West timber towns. The wilderness might also function as a space for recreation, but its core function is to provide resources that rugged men can reap to provide for their families.

The New West, by contrast, sees the natural environment as a space to escape the perceived or manufactured realities of some other place, a place that is more crowded or less safe. In this postextractive economy, the natural landscape itself is the product (not the trees that might be harvested). Packaging that landscape for maximum profit becomes the primary goal in the New West, especially for developments such as Mill Lake, where the primary draw for new residents is (controlled and manufactured) access to nature and natural beauty. Trees are still commodified in the New West, but in very different ways.

This shifting vision of nature has driven much of the change in the American West and has intensified since the 1980s and '90s. At the same time that neoliberalism, mechanization, and globalization were transforming extractive industries in the region, the supposedly endless American West began to feel limited. The interstate freeway system began to open up the West starting in the 1950s, allowing people to traverse the landscape more freely over the decades.[9] At the same time, the growing environmental movement in the United States promoted conservation and recreation in the protected West. The number of animals listed as endangered species dramatically increased in the 1980s and '90s,[10] with the spotted owl highlighting the fragility of old-growth forests, reminding Americans that wild spaces were finite and vulnerable to development and growth.

Under different political or economic conditions, these changes could have reshaped the West in a variety of ways, but under capitalism, beautiful natural spaces began to be viewed as an increasingly important commodity, especially for the affluent. As Michael P. Malone and Richard W. Etulain note, "affluent Americans saw the vanishing wilderness as something they needed and could afford."[11] Rather than seeing the forests of the Pacific Northwest as raw materials to fuel the economy, those spaces became much-desired commodities, a means to demonstrate wealth and bourgeois values by recreating in nature rather than razing it.

Ironically, the destruction of these spaces via logging throughout the twentieth century created an opportunity for profit because the destructive logging practices fostered the perception of scarcity. After decades of clear-cutting and timber extraction, the idea that the wild spaces of the West were now a limited commodity made them even more valuable.

THE NEW DOVER

The transformation from Old West to New West—or bypassed West to booming West—meant a fairly radical shift in the uses and meanings of natural spaces in a town such as Dover. As mentioned in chapter 1, during the mill years in Dover, there was an openness and communality to land and space. Some of the oldest residents shared that, when they were children, most families kept a milk cow that was let out each morning after milking to graze the open lands around the town. The townsfolk hunted in the woods owned by the timber companies. They fished where the fish bit and swam where the beaches were sandy. Dover included large "common" lands that were owned by the mill owner but that people could freely use as long as they were following what they would likely call "common sense." The double meaning here of "common" is fitting: it was reasonable to have a cow to provide for your family and maybe a neighbor, or enough chickens to do the same, but it was understood that folks were not going to start a dairy farm using communal land.[12]

Of course, this communal use of space didn't extend to timber. If locals had chopped down trees owned by the mill, it likely would have caused an uproar. And the communal uses of the land also went hand in hand with extremely dangerous and demanding working conditions; the common spaces were a sort of bargain the timber companies made that helped keep the workers fed and happy but that required very little effort or capital on their part. This worked, since timber, and not the natural landscape, was the commodity at the time.

However, when natural spaces themselves become the primary commodity of the New West, these kinds of communal practices threatened these new economic relationships. People in Dover had not had a communal milking cow roaming the streets for a long time, but they certainly viewed spaces such as the beach and bluff as belonging to the community right up until the development was built. And the community's tension with the mill site owners began almost immediately after the mill closed and the value of the land as a development became the primary source of profit for the owners. Any eventual development would be selling access to nature, putting the developers in direct conflict with the openness found in old Dover.

It is ironic, then, that the Mill Lake development was pitched to the city council and the residents of Dover as a way to ensure *more* public spaces for the community. The threat of turning the development into a gated community or a golf course (however real) worried residents of old Dover, who desperately wanted open, accessible public spaces for both old and new Dover. And there is no doubt that the developer delivered on the promise of keeping Dover an open community. There are miles of paved trails for biking and running, a restaurant, a dog park, a public beach, and no gates. However, gates are only the most obvious way of separating communities. Barriers to social class can be just as effective.

While the Mill Lake development is open and offers a range of public spaces to all residents, old and new, the development restructures the spatial relationship between the community and nature, offering a simulated version of the Old West with the amenities and classed assumptions of the New West. The development packages nature and offers public access, but largely in constricted and highly structured ways: cement walking trails instead of open spaces to wander through, a marina instead of grassy beaches where anyone can launch a small boat, and commodified amenities like health clubs and spas to supplement the draw of the natural world. These changes reflect assumptions about social class, recreation, and nature. The development created new public spaces, but those reflect a narrow vision of public access based on a middle-class and affluent worldview.

These divisions are clear in the spatial organization of the community itself. You can't get to Mill Lake without driving through the north edge of old Dover on what used to be the highway. To access the new development, you have to pass by rows of tidy manufactured homes and the old saddle repair shop before Mill Lake Boulevard opens up.

Today, a boulevard divider lined with trees leads you toward the lake, roughly following the old mill road. The lake is the main draw, and the entrance to the community leads you to the lake, highlighting the beauty of North Idaho and asking people to imagine interacting with the lake and the wilderness. Old Dover has no part in this layout—it is simply the working-class waypoint one must pass to enter the sanctuary of the development.

Almost everyone agrees the development is beautiful, but its beauty is designed with its back to old Dover. Most of the houses in Mill Lake are literally turned away from the old community to face the lake or the new roads. The contrast between the old and new is also physical: old Dover is a series of disparate homes and trailers, while Mill Lake unfolds rows and rows of similarly designed buildings. Across the development, there is a striking sameness in the pitch and color of the new roofs, the unbroken lines of brown-gray structures, the manicured lawns surrounded by white picket fences, and the rows of leafy trees.

The symmetry is deliberate, as is the development's attempt to give the new buildings a rustic, natural feel. The designer who oversaw the project encourages people to look at Mill Lake from the top of the bluff to get a full sense of it. He said, "We wanted to design guidelines, [to] control roof and roof color. . . . We wanted to have as much of the historic

6.1. A view down an original street in Dover. The power lines and lack of sidewalks are hallmarks of this neighborhood that has remained relatively unchanged for decades.

materials work with the architectural components—real wood. . . . For the most part, there's a real earnest push to try to look at [natural] products, real materials." And even the residents of old Dover who resisted the development are some of the first to admit that the new development is beautiful and meticulously planned.

But this deliberate planning sets the world of new Dover apart from that of old Dover, often reflecting the very different assumptions underpinning each community. In old Dover, the streets are arranged in a traditional grid system, with the north-south streets numbered and the east-west streets named for presidents. The layout reflects the nineteenth- and early twentieth-century ideologies around people imposing rigid order on the natural world. By contrast, the roads in Mill Lake are meant to interact with and reflect the contours of the landscape. The roads curve

6.2. A view down the main boulevard in the Mill Lake development, where sidewalks are flanked by white picket fences and the houses follow a very similar design.

around natural hills and snake around the edges of the wetlands. As a result, the spaces of old and new Dover seem to exist on different planes, visible to one another and yet difficult to navigate between.

These design differences, of course, are a result of very different building practices and environmental regulations. As the land planner for the development noted, when Dover was built, "you could fill [wetlands], you could do a number of things to really get a grid pattern. That was really the formulation of our cities." But by 2004, building was a very different process, one that required wetland assessment and other environmental impact reports. Ever optimistic, the land planner said that "one of the beauties of [Mill Lake] is that a lot of the wetland determinations really started to define the open space and the character of it. A lot of times on the hilltops and so forth, we really didn't want to develop, although that would be a prime area from a planning standpoint. It's really not a good plan."

The development, however, is not simply designed to highlight the natural beauty of the space; it is designed to monetize that beauty. The land planner notes that the plan for Mill Lake "looks at everything as market-driven . . . [In Mill Lake] there's a complete diversity of housing types, sizewise, expensewise, based on resources and views, exposures. All of those kinds of things start to determine a price point for the product." The location of lots, their views, their size, are all assigned value as commodities, and the development parceled out the space to reach a variety of price points. Expansive views and access to more natural space yielded higher-end lots and homes, while condos farther from the lake yielded more affordable middle-class options. The natural beauty of the mill site, in other words, has been carefully assessed and dissected to maximize the commodities offered to consumers.

This parceling of the natural spaces into commodities extends to the kinds of amenities built into the development. The former mill site is now divided into thirteen unique neighborhoods with names designed to evoke the natural beauty of the space ("Cabins in the Woods" and "Dover Meadows," for example), but access to nature in the development is mediated through the manufactured amenities that the development provides. According to the Mill Lake website, these amenities include "more than 9 miles of trails along the water and through natural preserves, an exceptional community beach, 150 acres of park area, a 274-slip marina, and Marina Village featuring a market, café, and fitness club." Marketers for the development also encourage canoeing in the wetlands, motorboating on the lake and river (you can rent boats at the development's marina), and skiing at the local ski mountain in the wintertime.

The website for the development is an almost perfect distillation of what "amenity migration" looks like for gentrifying rural communities, rattling off expansive lists of recreational opportunities for those lucky enough to live there. According to the website, Mill Lake guarantees "four seasons of fun and irreplaceable natural amenities."

The marketing of the natural world by the development was made explicit one afternoon while Larry Davis, a resident of old Dover, was out for a bike ride with his grandson. The two were taking a break near the wooden bridges over the remaining wetlands close to "Goose-Shit Beach." According to Davis, "along comes a realtor with his ducklings [prospective homeowners] behind him. He looked across the swamp, and there's a cow moose with her calf." The realtor shushed the group and declared, "That's what we call a [Mill Lake] moment!" to the excited crowd, reinforcing the seeming exoticism of the landscape for the out-of-town visitors. But Davis chuckled at the marketing of the moose. "You know how dangerous moose are," he said. "You walk over there and [you'll] find out what a [Mill Lake] moment [really] is." While beautiful, the moose along the carefully cultivated trails are a very real source of danger. "I don't want [be] riding a bicycle past [a] moose or two," Davis declared.

If old Dover was about producing, Mill Lake is about consuming, specifically consuming the natural world. The trails, parks, and the public beach in the Mill Lake development are spaces that encourage residents to commodify their relationship to the land by "doing" outdoor recreation. Moreover, this consumption reflects a set of classed assumptions about the kinds of recreation that are most appropriate in this space. For example, on their website, Mill Lake includes a media gallery with a "lifestyle" tab. Of the dozen or so images that include people, they are all interacting with the environment through some activity that requires both expensive gear and the leisure time to pursue it. In these photos, we see people downhill skiing, jet skiing, paddling canoes, kayaks, and paddleboards. There weren't even any images of more "working-class" recreational activities that still require large investments, such as ATV riding or fishing. Mill Lake instead is designed with a specific social class in mind.

These suggested leisure activities are also designed with certain kinds of bodies in mind. Being capable of downhill skiing during retirement, for example, suggests you've led such a life that your body allows you to ski in your sixties or seventies. More than likely, you will have not fallen off a roof during a construction job or damaged your knee by using it to open the door between a kitchen and a dining room as a server thousands of times over the course of a lifetime. Retirement skiing suggests that you can access high-quality health care if you were to break a leg and that you have likely conditioned your body through regular exercise because you are not too exhausted to do so after working a physically demanding job.

To that end, today there is a fitness center with a pool and hot tub where the old mill once sat. Social class is, in part, maintained through the body, with a fit body acting as a sign that someone has the time, money, and cultural capital to walk into a fitness center. In essence, to work out is to use your body to burn calories and time, with the goal of not producing anything that can be shared—not food, or heat, or a wage—but instead to produce a fit body.

The fitness center also marks a clear difference in how bodies in the Old and New West are understood. In the Old West, for both men and women, good bodies were those that were strong, where strength was realized in physical doing. Could you catch a fish, plant a garden, chop wood? In the New West, especially for women, a trim body is a marker of class: it is a body that doesn't jiggle or take up too much space. The regimes of exercise (having the time to exercise, accessing sleek exercise clothing, affording access to fitness centers) have become a particularly important means of being seen consuming and interacting with nature in the New West.

Particularly in Dover, boats were also key in clarifying the different forms of recreating and interacting with nature across social class. Whether motorboats, pontoon boats, canoes, or kayaks, in interview after interview, boats came up as a reason to live in Mill Lake. Many of the people I interviewed in the development kept a boat at the marina, which included nearly three hundred slips (the equivalent of a reserved parking stall for a boat), nearly all of them full. The price to rent one started at over a $1,000 for the May-to-September season. People who had a slip could be on the water in mere minutes, walking from their front door straight to their boat. They didn't have to worry about waiting to back up a trailer to the water and paying a fee to launch. For these residents, boats were about recreation and leisure.

For residents of old Dover, however, boats were for fishing: recreation in the service of (or perhaps under the auspices of) producing. Boats were a source of some of the deepest feelings of contention voiced by older residents who claimed the developer promised them they would be able to launch their boats for free; instead, once Mill Lake was finished, launching a boat came with a $25 price tag. Since there are no records of the meetings, these residents cannot prove anything (though there is mention of this promise in a newspaper article).[13] Regardless, the older residents mostly fish off the docks of the marina, though the right to do that was under threat too, since the developer (who also owns the marina) claimed that fishers were leaving a mess on the docks.

For those in Dover who just want to launch an old fishing boat, the launch fee is part of a larger set of cultural changes that have transformed the town. Amenity migration reorganizes rural space for consumption, transforming relatively open and unregulated spaces into more controlled spaces where nature has been packaged for consumption and monetized.

Gene Nelson, who had lived in Dover long enough that he could remember trading with the Kalispel people who would set up their summer camp close to Dover, noted that the physical change in Dover was beautiful: "All honesty, it's beautiful compared to what—big sawdust piles and—really, the paths and stuff is—it's much nicer than just having big sawdust piles there and nothing there." However, he lamented the losses that the residents of old Dover felt: "[By] the same token, you can't use the property there anymore. We used to go down and fish off the bluff down there. You can't do that anymore, because people's got houses built all over."

These spatial transformations create very real barriers across social classes, as the spaces of the New West are organized to suit the leisure and recreation needs of the affluent. Dover may have avoided a gated community, but the restructuring of space along class divisions has created its own kinds of gates and walls.

ENVIRONMENTALISM IN THE NEW WEST

The changes that have found their way to Dover and other rural communities in the West, however, are often touted as being more environmentally sensitive. While developments such as Mill Lake might reflect divisions in social class between the newcomers and the old-timers, the design of the development (and the leisure activities that places like Mill Lake encourage) are often seen as being easier on the natural world. Especially compared to the environmentally devastating practices of extractive industries in the West over the past 150 years—from clear-cutting to strip mining—the changes wrought by amenity migration often seem to represent a more ethical form of environmental stewardship, inviting people to appreciate the natural world on their kayaks rather than felling trees and producing chemical-intensive wood products in mills.

However, just as the amenities of the New West create class-based boundaries between newcomers and old-timers, environmental rhetoric often reflects the assumptions of the affluent. In Dover, moreover, the fallout of Mill Lake's supposedly ecologically sound design often meant that a bigger burden was placed on the shoulders of the working-class old-timers, furthering divisions in the town.

As the developers in Dover blew up the bluff to lay foundations for homes, filled wetlands to build roads, and cut towering trees to clear the land for condos, they claimed that they, in fact, were the true environmental stewards of the land. The land planner for Mill Lake pointed out that "we did environmental impact, wetlands assessment, so many other previous studies to really look at this from an environmental impact." These assessments, he argues, fostered a responsive design for the development that worked with the natural landscape instead of demolishing it to make way for new buildings and roads. Environmental protection was at the center of Mill Lake, from this perspective.

Of course, as many scholars have noted, amenity migration and new developments often bring with them serious environmental concerns. More roads mean more runoff, more houses mean less open space, and more lawns mean more herbicides.[14] This is not to deny that the land planner and other designers for Mill Lake weren't responsive to environmental concerns. However, these designs were put in place to mitigate the increased population along the river, which would invariably put more stress on the ecology of the old mill site. Being sensitive to the environment may have been a factor in the design of the development, but it was not so important that the developers questioned the environmental impact of expanding the population of Dover (and the profits that could be reaped from such an expansion).

Additionally, the environmental assessments conducted by the development were not optional considerations that ethical developers could choose to undertake. They were required by law. But as the residents of old Dover found out, legally mandated environmental regulations do not necessarily protect communities from the whims of developers as much as they provide avenues for developers to legally pass responsibility or consequences onto those without the same legal recourse as large, well-funded entities.

For example, as I discussed in chapter 4, the developers of Mill Lake navigated around restrictions on filling wetlands with a solution that fit the letter of the law but perhaps not its spirit. The development was only allowed to fill in up to a tenth of an acre of wetlands, but, to make more room for more units and more profit, the developer allowed each individual lot owner to also fill in up to a tenth of an acre to build a home, a seeming loophole in the regulations. This tactic certainly calls into question the assertion that Mill Lake put the environment at the center of its planning, but it also shows how developers can pass along responsibility to others.

As more and more homeowners in Mill Lake began filling in small sections of wetland, but en masse, the impact of filling wetlands in the development was that an old-timer's horse pasture became a wetland. The water in these newly filled-in former wetlands needed somewhere to go, so it headed upstream to the pasture. Now the old-timer has a wetland on his property. And because this new wetland is the culmination of many small fills upstream (that didn't require permitting), it's too large for him to fill in without requiring *him* to get a permit from the Army Corps of Engineers.

Complaints about the Environmental Protection Agency from old-timers may seem like a general antienvironmentalist complaint, but this example suggests the reality of many environmental regulations: they are designed to protect our watersheds but sometimes end up allowing developers to skirt the rules, leaving the guy upstream to feel the full force their impact.

Government regulations also seemed to impact the old-timers more than the developers when it came to the banks of the river. As the development took shape, the developer was required to conduct an archaeological investigation of the site, since the marina he'd proposed would result in significant motorboat traffic on the river. The wakes from these boats would then create substantial increases in wave action against the banks of the river, eroding them and endangering any of the Indigenous artifacts the land was cradling. The small sample of sites along the riverside that were excavated produced dozens of artifacts from the Kalispel people.[15] To avoid washing away these cultural artifacts, Mill Lake Development was required to shore up the banks of the Pend Oreille River with riprap (a foundation or sustaining wall of stones or chunks of concrete).

Once the riprap was in place, however, there was no longer a gently sloping shoreline from which to launch a small fishing boat. For the first time in nearly a century, residents could no longer back their fishing boats into the river whenever it pleased them. Instead, launching a tiny fishing boat in Dover now means playing the Mill Lake marina $25. For these residents, government regulations didn't mean cleaner water or a healthier community—it meant the further commodification of the natural resources that they had used for generations.

Too often, then, people embraced an overly simplistic understanding of newcomer and old-timers in the changing American West, assuming that working-class residents don't care about the environment, what with their ax-hacking of the trees and industrial timber mills. Newcomers, on the other hand, are assumed to value the open spaces of the natural world and are good at sorting their recycling. As a result of these assumptions, working-class people are increasingly pushed out of conversations about how the land can and should be used.

But this was not always the case. In *Empire of Timber*, Erik Loomis carefully outlines the complex relationship between timber unions and environmental activism. According to him, loggers played a key role in protecting forests throughout the twentieth century as unions—in addition to advocating for better working conditions and pay—also demanded that timber companies develop sustainable harvesting strategies that would protect the long-term health of the forest. The loggers saw healthy forests as key to the long-term survival of their labor and their communities, rightly understanding the impact of unfettered capitalism on workers and the environment.[16]

It was only in the late 1970s and early 1980s that these relationships changed. As timber workers became increasingly expendable because of rapid automation and changing global markets, lumber companies began to use environmental protections as a cover for eliminating jobs. It was much easier to blame the growing environmental movement in the United States for job losses, deflecting responsibility from timber companies' changing business practices that came at the expense of working families. The goals of this tactic were obvious to "many workers [who] felt that corporations blamed environmentalists for plants they intended to close."[17] Loomis quotes a logger, Bruce Miller, who accused his employer of using "environmentalists as a 'whipping boy to get us workers in a fret,' and distract them from how corporate greed had led to unemployment."[18]

But the tactic bore fruit over the long haul, as timber unions and the working class in general bought into arguments that restrictive environmental regulations cost people jobs and devastated rural communities. It did not hurt that the government sometimes fostered animosity between labor unions and the environmental movement. For example, in the 1980s, unions and environmentalists worked together to pressure California into passing a law mandating significant payments to timber workers who were left unemployed after logging was stopped in the redwood forests. But the Reagan administration stepped in to stop those payments precisely to limit the ability of labor and environmentalists to find common solutions, according to Loomis.[19]

All the while, the mainstream environmental movement in the United States in this period often turned its back on working-class people, becoming more aligned with the worldview of the affluent. The legacy of these cultural shifts is certainly felt in Dover, where "environmentalism" seems to be a primary cause of tension between old Dover and the development. Issues such as the wetlands and the riprap on the riverbank make it seem like environmental regulations are the problem (and not the developer's responses to those regulations). However, the real tension here is not between working-class folks who don't care about the environment and newcomers who do but rather between working-class people who care deeply about their community and a vision of "environmental protection" that privileges those with money and certain forms of cultural capital. The old-timers care about natural spaces in the community and having access to them, but the kinds of cultivated access provided by the development are very different from the ways that the old-timers have traditionally used spaces such as the beach. In this way, the working-class old-timers often feel excluded from the world of Mill Lake, its amenities, and its vision of the natural environment.

And of course they *have* been excluded. As more and more newcomers arrive in Mill Lake, the worldview of the old-timers has less and less sway in important decision-making in the community. As Greg Clendenning, Donald R. Field, and Kirsten J. Kapp note, "It is important to understand the dynamics of second-home construction, not only because of the impacts on the land, but also because second-home owners are increasingly influential in land use and planning decisions in rural areas."[20] Newcomers in Mill Lake, in other words, held increasing influence on future land decisions, zoning decisions, and other important matters in the community, legitimizing and institutionalizing the vision of "environmental protection" that filled wetlands and dynamited the bluff but made it easier for them to bicycle down to the lake. The newcomers are now the new stewards of Dover's environment.

The logic of the Mill Lake development, however, is organized not around protecting the environment but monetizing it. The purpose of "protecting" natural spaces via amenity migration is to transform them into profitable commodities. And in the New West, environmental protections enhance the value of natural spaces by making them scarcer. As Paul Lorah and Rob Southwick note, "Those in favor of protecting federal lands claim that the presence of roadless areas and wilderness benefits local economies and leads to population growth."[21] This assertion has been borne out in the New West, where natural beauty is *the* draw because of the perceived scarcity of "nature."

Under the logic of capitalism, the solution to scarcity is to buy it up more quickly, creating a feedback loop whereby each acre that is bought makes the next acre more valuable. And as each acre becomes more valuable as a commodity, it becomes more apparent that those with wealth deserve those natural spaces because they will "protect" them from working-class rural folks who don't care about the environment. Developers certainly didn't invent this logic; they simply are the people with the resources and disposition to exploit it.

If this is what "environmentalism" looks like in the New West, it is hardly surprising that working-class rural communities have turned their backs on it.

CONCLUSION

Any critiques of the development in Dover, of course, are batted away by appeals to the rights of property owners: the land is private property, so the owners can do what they want with it. This argument was made explicit by a new resident who owned one of the lakefront homes. She said, "Before [Mill Lake], they used to go wherever and call it their own, but it was always private property. . . . [A] big part of the development being allowed was to make sure that public spaces were a part of that. [That's] huge. I mean, we have acres of public spaces. Everybody's welcome." Later in the interview, she reiterated the point, noting, "This always was private property. I think people forget that too, that just because they could come on here doesn't mean that would always be the case."

The idea that this was "always private property," however, is deeply historically inaccurate. For at least 98 percent of the time that humans have called this region home, the idea of "private property" was anathema to the spatial organization of Indigenous communities. And, if not for colonial settlers, this Indigenous perspective on land ownership may have been sustainable for another ten thousand years.

It was not until the late nineteenth century that the land on which Dover would be built would become "private property," and it became that way because it was seized by force and then given to large corporate interests. But even then, because the value of that property was defined by the resources that could be extracted from it, the idea of "private property" meant something very different. Residents of old Dover certainly wouldn't expect to profit off the land owned by the mills or others, but "private property" didn't necessarily equate to "no trespassing." It was only when the natural beauty of the land became the commodity that it became important to limit and control access to these spaces. The magnanimous gesture of providing walking trails and designated public spaces in the development only registers as a "gift" if one accepts the spatial logic of the New West.

Yet, the changes that amenity migration has brought to the rural West are supposed to be accepted as a natural fact of life, an inevitable form of progress. Even the terms scholars use—"Old to New West" or "dwindling to booming West"—imply a kind of evolutionary narrative in which things improve over time. This language suggests that communities that are "dwindling" should strive to "boom." These terms obscure the intentionality and agency exercised by wealthy individuals and corporations across this history to shape the landscape in very particular ways that benefit them. Dover exists because of intentional choices: railroad and timber industrialists could create huge profits in these places because the federal government essentially gave them huge tracts of land. And Dover declined because of a similar logic: when logging in those spaces became less profitable, timber companies invested in mechanization and consolidated the industry, leaving only a handful of mills in operation in the region. Calling Dover "new" or "booming" has the potential to erase this history and obscure how this change came at the expense of the people who had carefully built lives in Dover.

The Mill Lake community itself is also not "natural" or a sign of progress. It was designed in a very specific way to maximize its marketability and profitability by embodying a set of class-based assumptions about how someone is supposed to interact with and appreciate the natural world. Its design was deliberate, with millions of dollars invested in the physical transformation of the community to attract the Patagonia-wearer and the recently retired. When we lose track of the history of this space, it is easy to see the development as simply the way things are. However, despite the public spaces, the walking trails, the public beach, and the assurances from the newcomers that "everybody's welcome," Mill Lake had fundamentally and deliberately reorganized the community in ways that leave old-timers on the outside, looking in.

7

A Tale of Two Dovers

THE DOVER I remember from my youth in the 1990s was dotted with piles of sawdust covering acres of the mill site. The sawdust gave off a piney, earthy smell and was also perfect cover for games like "chess." An early precursor to paint-gun battles, chess was a euphemistically named strategy game played on the bluff and around the sawdust piles, in which local teens, often wearing old military fatigues and helmets, would attempt to shoot each other with BB guns. A stray BB was the reason that a friend attended her senior prom sporting a large bruise on her forehead that had aged to yellowish green by the time we took pictures. Another friend has carried a BB around in his tongue for twenty years.

In those years, the mill site was an open and somewhat wild place where children rode bikes on the dirt roads and teenagers brazenly continued partying at "Dover Beach." Despite increasingly strident warnings against trespassing, the beach and bluff continued to be favorite spots for the community. And we mostly got used to stepping over the thick cable wire that closed off the old mill road or slipping past the post that held it up.

Like generations before us, the mill site and surrounding land was a space where young and old alike could find both solitude and camaraderie. When another friend lost both her parents in the space of six months, we were far too young to know how to mourn such a tragedy. So we turned to the shores of the river. Walking farther down the old mill road than we had ever gone before, secretly daring the watchman to disrupt our raw grief, we found a quiet spot on the river to drop flowers into the water for her parents and mourn with her. That day, all we found was quiet.

There are so many ways to measure the change in rural communities in the face of amenity migration, but do they account for the loss of camaraderie and community cohesion? We can compare the price of housing or the number of people who have come and gone. We can measure the jobs created and what those jobs pay. We can devise elaborate pro-and-con lists and tables. These are fine ways to measure change (and ones that will inform this chapter), but how can you measure the friendships that never form when there are no more spaces for children to roam free and break rules? How can you measure the relationships that never solidify because people do not come together in public spaces in the ways they used to? How can you measure the grief that remains bottled up because there are no quiet places to mourn?

These elusive but important components of the community are etched in the old photos from the 1930s on display in the Dover community hall, the photos I discussed at the start of this book: little boys in coveralls and girls in simple dresses, their names scrawled underneath each picture. It was startling to have interviewed people now in their nineties and then see their faces peering out of the photos as small children. For those residents, the freedom and mischief-making of old Dover made the community special. Two of the little boys in those class photos, now old men, regaled me with tales of their youth from nearly eighty years ago and then swore me to secrecy. They were happy to speak on the record about how they felt about the development, but I had to promise that one prank, in particular, would stay between us. These memories are what make a town a community, and for many, the new development brought an end to secret pranks, picnics at the beach, games of "chess," and all the other interactions that were fostered by the open spaces of old Dover.

This chapter attempts to articulate this indefinable sense of loss. Instead of measuring our world with coffee spoons—parsing out the changes in median home prices or average wages and pretending that that is what makes a community function—I want to explore instead how the new development has transformed the sense of community and belonging in the new, divided Dover. How has the development transformed the life and culture of Dover?

This is not to say that Dover hasn't gained anything from the development. Its population has grown—and is still growing—bringing in some new jobs and new opportunities for people. Additionally, as I discussed in the previous chapter, almost everyone acknowledges that the development did a good job of creating new public spaces, including walking trails, parks, and a public beach. And while the beach isn't the one the community fought for, it is still a small slice of public waterfront in a region where waterfront property is exorbitantly expensive. A few miles upstream, another former mill site turned suburban neighborhood keeps its community beach behind lock and key, with a stern sign reminding people that the beach is for homeowners only. The old-timers' worst fear—an exclusive, gated community—was certainly avoided in Dover.

Both the developer and the old-timers try to take credit for these concessions to community cohesion. Dover old-timers who served on the city council insist that their pressure on the developer ensured amenities such as the walking trails and the public beach, while the developers claim that those were their ideas from the get-go, that they had always valued shared public spaces.[1]

But the public spaces that were so clearly valued by residents meant very different things to them than to the developer. Dover old-timers hoped that those spaces, along with the new economic opportunities that came with the development, might at least resemble the community and camaraderie of the past. They cared about the beach and the bluff not just because they were beautiful and worthy of protection but because their lives intersected with friends, neighbors, and loved ones in those spaces. For them, Dover was about their connections with one another and their pride in having helped create the community. With the dream of a new mill (and with it, new working-class jobs) long dead and buried, the old-timers hoped that the development might at least bring people and new connections, maybe new picnics at the community hall that could be commemorated in photos that would hang for another eighty years. The old-timers certainly didn't "choose" the development, but—given the range

7.1. Some of the miles of public trails in Mill Lake that highlight the natural beauty of the area that encouraged Mill Lake residents to move here.

of options that could have doomed their community—they at least held hopes that a sense of community cohesion might be restored.

The results, however, have been mixed so far, often leaving Dover old-timers disillusioned. This chapter explores several key areas where community cohesion has been threatened, reinforcing the sense of loss experienced by residents of old Dover. For example, while the population of Dover is growing, the development has increased a sense of intergenerational displacement and failed to provide the kinds of working-class jobs that could give the families of residents of old Dover a future in the new community. Dover is no longer a community where multiple generations live alongside one another. Moreover, the influx of newcomers into the town has created more community strife than cohesion, as differences in social class often keep the town divided.

These changes, of course, are no fault of the newcomers who have arrived in Dover, who are generally lovely people who want to be a part of a successful community themselves. But the changes brought by the development itself—from its impact on property values to the demographics it attracts—often provide concrete hurdles to a sense of common identity for old and new Dover.

This chapter asks the reader to understand these changes in Dover as a logical consequence of an economic system that reorganizes space and social relations with the interests of those with economic power in mind. This system necessitates the destruction of not only space and landscape but of older communities, which are replaced with others organized around vastly different values.

In this chapter, I show how the process of building Mill Lake meant also the building of laws and regulations for reorganizing the economy around the economic interests of the developer and the residents of Mill Lake. From laws that outlawed "junk" in yards to the loss of well-paid working-class jobs, this chapter considers how Mill Lake was built in a way to benefit development.

INTERGENERATIONAL DISPLACEMENT

The residents who became resigned to the idea of development hoped that the future of Dover might somewhat resemble the community they had known in the past. Throughout the process, they pushed hard for a development with shared open spaces, hopeful that old Dover and new Dover might interact, re-creating something of the vibrancy of the past, full of social events and friendly neighbors.

Old Dover, after all, had been slowly shedding residents and loved ones to the surrounding area. John White, who was one of the very few people his age who'd grown up in Dover and remained after the development, detailed how the community changed as he listed who had left. Two of his friends stayed in Bonner County, he said, noting that "they're mainly [doing] construction, handyman stuff," while his sister works at the local salad dressing company. Most of the rest—a brother, a sister, and loads of friends—have left the region for the oil fields of North Dakota, or for medical work in Seattle, or anywhere else they can make a living. His friend Tanya is "a union flagger. She's got the life of a gypsy." His cousin who grew up next door "works in Portland. He manages a rechroming plant." Another neighbor and friend is in Oregon working in property management.

He continued his list, sharing how he was generating so many names: "I'm just thinking about school bus drops." Who was left from all the children of Dover who rode the school bus with him? When I mention that he has seen a lot of leaving, he agreed: "Most of 'em did because . . . there wasn't much there. Low wages."

For residents who had grown up in Dover, surrounded by family, these losses made the prospect of the development seem moderately appealing as it was being debated in the city council. More people could mean more activity, more hubbub around town, and an end to the uncanny quiet that had gripped the community since the mill closed. But while the development would bring more people into Dover, it also set up barriers for many people who would want to make it their home, including the working-class family members of the residents of old Dover.

Old-time residents still call Dover home, but, unlike their parents and grandparents, they are not neighbored by generations of their family members, and it seems likely that they will be the last generation of their families to reside there. As Sharon Miller explained, "All three of my kids don't like Dover anymore. They don't like the way it is. It's beautiful, don't get me wrong, but it still isn't old Dover. We had so much fun. In the winter, we'd play, groups of us would play cards for fun." Her family still lives in the area, but not in Dover, a stark contrast to her youth, when she grew up alongside siblings, cousins, and friends (some of whom would become family after they married each other), creating a web of relationships that made everyone in Dover like a sort of extended family.

For Sharon's children and other relatives of those who resided in old Dover, the decision to live elsewhere wasn't simply about personal choices: they were priced out. There are still lots for sale in the Mill Lake development, advertised on billboards along the highway or listed in upscale real estate magazines, imploring people to "try life at the lake." But a 0.8-acre lot in the "Estuary Forest" neighborhood of the new development can cost $195,000. According to the development's website, a lakefront home by the bluff runs nearly two million dollars.

These are lots and homes designed to encourage affluent migrants to move to the area, not to provide housing opportunities for lower-middle-class or working-class families. The development, of course, does offer a variety of price points and kinds of homes, including more affordable condos. Mill Lake is not simply for the uberwealthy, which is a welcome change from other kinds of new developments in the West. But even the lower-end units in the development are well above the price range of many working families.

Additionally, as a result of the development, the price of older homes in Dover has also rapidly increased. A modest two-bedroom manufactured home is estimated to cost $200,000, and property taxes increased on some older homes in Dover by as much as 60 percent between 2017 and 2019 alone.[2] And some of these homes are being bought up and remodeled, with modular and modern-looking "old" homes now sitting in between the traditional mill workers' homes, further increasing average home costs in old Dover. So even if the families of residents wanted to buy in old Dover instead of the development, those options are increasingly expensive and out of reach.

This even includes adding new buildings to existing property owned by residents of old Dover. One family who lived on a big lot had a granddaughter who had wanted to put a trailer house on her family's property, allowing her to live next to her grandparents. The cost to connect to the sewer alone was $15,000, so she put her trailer about twenty miles north.

These price increases are a common feature of rural gentrification and fuel a stark sense of intergenerational displacement in many rural communities across the rural West. As prices are driven up, older residents are locked into the homes they bought decades earlier, while also typically facing higher property taxes. Their children and grandchildren, then, are pushed out of the community because they can no longer afford housing there and because there aren't any good jobs in the area that can support the cost of housing. For many rural communities, the hallmark of amenity migration is an intergenerational loss as housing prices rapidly increase.[3]

To be fair, the kinds of economic stagnation for middle- and working-class families in the bypassed West also produce their own forms of intergenerational displacement. A lack of jobs and economic opportunities in rural communities often means that young people are forced to seek out new prospects elsewhere, often in more populous areas of the "booming" West or in far-flung big cities. This was certainly the case in Dover after the mill closed but before the development, when there was really no future for many young people in Dover. The young Dover residents that I came of age with in the 1990s, for example, are now dispersed across the region.

These population losses then further devalue land in the bypassed West, making it vulnerable to development, depending on its scenic value, because it has been starved of economic opportunities for the middle class and working class. Developments offer the prospect of population growth but not a solution for intergenerational displacement, often making it even harder for young people who were raised in these areas to make their lives in their hometowns.

As this suggests, another key factor in this kind of intergenerational displacement is jobs. Development is often sold to communities as an economic rising tide that will lift all boats. More people, including the affluent, will mean more services needed in the community, which will mean more jobs for everyone, across social class. But there is no evidence in Dover of this being the case. The Mill Lake development has created a new community for amenity migrants who seek a refuge in their retirement or who are fleeing from career burnout, but the jobs created by the development have been few, and often organized around meeting the needs of amenity migrants. These service-sector jobs are often not the kinds that can sustain families.

Service-sector jobs, after all, hardly pay well, especially in states, such as Idaho, with a low minimum wage ($7.25 an hour) and even lower minimum wages for servers ($3.35 an hour, with the expectation that tips will raise your pay to minimum wage). If you answer a Craigslist ad for a job at the restaurant in Dover, you'll learn that they "pay $4 an hour plus tips." But they assure potential employees that "we are a very busy restaurant, so if you are skilled at your job, the money is very good."[4] The restaurant in Dover is typically open four months a year, however, so an employee would have to find another job in the fall, winter, and spring.

In a town driven by amenity migration, most employment is seasonal as well as being gendered. Men end up in landscaping, women end up serving at restaurants or cleaning houses or watching the kids of the families working in these jobs. In the fall, when the wind picks up and the rain starts, lakeside restaurants close and landscapers find themselves without lawns to mow. Everyone in these seasonal jobs is at the mercy of the snow. If it comes early, they can work at the ski mountain or plow driveways. But nothing is guaranteed, and some years the ski mountain doesn't open until mid-December and there's not much snow to move.

Service-sector jobs also guarantee that you'll be working every weekend and every holiday. If you have a partner who works regular business hours or if you have children in school, there's a good chance you'll be like ships passing in the night. The same holds for construction jobs, which are also touted as an important economic boon created by developments. But these jobs are hard, physical jobs that also require rigid work schedules. One Mill Lake resident noted these harsh working conditions when observing construction on a neighboring house. Workers had been building the house "in this terrible weather on ladders," he noted, every day throughout the holiday season except Christmas.

These are also not the kinds of jobs that will ensure economic stability for one's family or one's future. John White—the middle-aged man who grew up in Dover and who could rattle off the names of a dozen friends who had left town—said that my job as a professor is what he would call a "retirement job." If I put in my time, I could expect to spend the final years of my life not working. With the loss of unionized timber jobs, he and most of the Doverites he grew up with would probably never have access to such jobs. White's off-handed comment about his "retirement job" further exemplifies the barriers between old Dover and Mill Lake. The new residents that communities in the booming West attract are often retired amenity migrants, but the ability to retire has become increasingly out of reach for the working class. Mill Lake has created an opportunity for affluent retirees to enjoy nature in the place that John called home, but for working-class folks like him, even the idea of retirement is increasingly out of reach.

Given these kinds of economic "opportunities," it is no wonder that young people are displaced and leave the area. For the working class that had watched their communities grow and thrive as a result of extractive economies, this is a painful transition. Economic stagnation meant that parents would watch their grown children—who couldn't afford to buy homes or raise their own children or retire in Dover—leave the area. And then the only lifeline offered to such communities—in the form of development and amenity migration—only exacerbated the economic precarity of this working class, who had called Dover home for generations. In both cases, the kind of intergenerational community that these residents valued have become near impossibilities.

For the old-timers of Dover, though, the one consolation has been the return of something that has been missing from Dover for years: children. Mill Lake is mostly temporary residents and retirees, but thanks to the growth in the town, some of the new remodels in old Dover have become homes again for young families with children. The residents of old Dover had hoped to grow old next door to their grandchildren, but the return of the sounds of *any* children playing in the streets are a welcome addition to the community.

COMMUNITY COHESION?

Despite the increasing activity in Dover, for many residents of old Dover, the development didn't deliver on its promises of a better community. Sam Lenn, whose beloved wife Sandy was the only vote against the development on the old city council, told me that, "[in terms of] quality of life," he says, "[we've gained] nothing." One of his neighbors agreed: "Have we gained anything? A lotta people."

But there is a difference between people and a community. After the development was built, old and new Dover struggled to come together as a cohesive community, often failing to live up to the hopes of residents of old Dover who yearned for the old days of a vibrant, social world.

A major contribution to these struggles was the demographics of Mill Lake. Only a handful of property owners in the development were full-time residents. The number varied, but most stakeholders put the figure at about only 25 percent. It seems ironic that the larger the home, the more likely it was to be sitting empty.

Beatrice Adams, who had served as the city clerk during the transition, noted, "The people that live in new Dover, there's very few live there full-time, so it's very transitory. Then you have the old mill town that's very community orientated, and so it doesn't blend well."

Of course, the residents of Mill Lake who do make it their permanent home were equally anxious to become integrated into the existing Dover community. I found plenty of gracious Mill Lake residents who welcomed me into their condos and small homes, carefully decorated and almost always including a large, friendly dog. These were all not far from the lake or river; none lived in any of the massive waterfront mansions. Some residents had views of the water but noted that they were temporary: soon more condos would be built and obscure the view.

These more permanent Mill Lake residents were largely retired from white-collar jobs. (Presumably, the 75 percent of homes that sit empty much of the year are second homes for people with careers that demand their attention elsewhere, the house in Mill Lake being an incentive to keep at that job.) These newcomers had vacationed either on the lake or the ski mountain (or both) for years. When it came time to imagine the next chapter of their lives, the memories of Sandpoint or the mountains called to them. For others, it was a recommendation at a far-flung bar or from a friend that brought them to the area to check out what it had to offer. Mill Lake featured nearly everything they were looking for in their retirement: opportunities to stay active on miles of trails, picturesque views, and a price they could afford. And, in an oft-repeated line, once they hit the Long Bridge, they knew (or at least hoped) they were home.

Perhaps because these residents identified the region as their new home, nearly all the people I interviewed in Mill Lake felt conflicted about the changes that they had helped bring about. The residents in Mill Lake's more modest offerings—still impressive by any standard but certainly not large waterfront homes—seemed empathetic to the changes in Dover and how it must feel to watch the community change. They often acknowledged and were uncomfortable with the economic inequalities between the two communities.

Thus, out of character for people sometimes termed "forever tourists," these newcomers had all thrown themselves into volunteering in the community. The organization where many of them met is one that raises money to give, without strings attached, to people in need: to buy backpacks and school supplies for local kids, to pay power bills in the winter, and to fill gas tanks for those who need cancer treatments and must travel out of state to receive them. The newcomers were also involved in political and other charitable organizations, and made a point of having dinners together.

In the home of one of these newcomers, historical images of the old Dover mill dotted the walls, as he had taken a keen interest in the history of the community and had volunteered at the historical society after his move to the area. Most of the documents at the historical society that I used to research the history of Dover were likely organized by this newcomer.

Despite some early efforts on the part of residents of both Mill Lake and old Dover, however, there's been essentially no social contact between the two groups. Most often, cultural barriers around social class keep the two communities separate.

One of those attempts to bring the two groups together was the annual Dover Picnic that has been part of the city's history for as long as anyone could remember. According to everyone I interviewed, trying to combine the two communities in one event didn't go well. While they all seemed to appreciate the opportunity to come together, there was a sort of barrier between the groups. The old residents sat at one set of tables, and the Mill Lake residents sat at different tables. I imagine that the former might have brought Jell-O salad, dinner rolls, and potato salad, while the latter brought a caprese salad and a baguette.

One of the new residents recalled the awkwardness of the last picnic: "It was kind of funny," he said, "because you could walk up [and] you could tell who was from [Mill Lake] and who was from Dover. The Dover people had their Carhartts on and their blue jeans, suspenders." But on the Mill Lake side, "the guy from San Diego had his polo shirt on and was there with his glass of wine. It was all the things that you would imagine would happen [at] something like that." He concluded, "They don't have those picnics anymore. They decided they were not as successful as they had hoped." A former city worker used the community picnic as an example of one of the more obvious changes in Dover. She listed "the old tradition of the picnic, the Dover picnic" as one of the things that "went by the wayside" after Dover was developed.

Differences in social class are also apparent in the new restaurant, touted by the developers as a boon for the community by bringing business into Mill Lake. The restaurant is downriver from the marina and overlooks the river. A group of women from Mill Lake meet there on occasion to catch up on what's happening in the community. Like nearly every restaurant in the region, the dress is casual, but the offerings—avocado fries, for example, or a $15 prosciutto and arugula salad—mark the restaurant as middle to upper class. Perhaps in a nod to the locals of old Dover, the most affordable meal on the menu is called "the Dover Burger." It's a simple cheeseburger with eyebrow-raising "dill pickle black pepper mayo," either a typo desperately in need of a comma or a spread desperately in need of a more restrained chef. Either way, while many of the older residents mentioned that it was nice to have a restaurant in the community, only a couple of people that I interviewed in old Dover had eaten there, and none of them regularly.

Other changes in the community also have left the residents of old Dover feeling left out or overlooked, such as the loss of certain freedoms and the rise of new city ordinances and regulations. For example, Mill Lake brought along with it a new set of codes for leashing dogs. Nearly every greeting from a new resident included an introduction to a dog: many of the new residents had gotten one when they retired, and Mill Lake is a dog paradise. But the number of dogs in the community brought increased scrutiny to both old and new residents. John White had grown up in old Dover and was one of the few residents who still had extended family in the community. In his typically colorful way, he noted that one of his biggest sources of frustration with the development was being told to leash his dogs. White noted: "I free-run my dogs . . . They will constantly say something about leash laws. I know that there's an unenforced leash law in Bonner County. At least I've heard that. I don't know it for a fact. I tell them to get bent. I say, 'I am not leashing my dogs. I'm running my dogs. I'm exercising my dogs. They're friendly dogs. They're family dogs.' I've got seven kids and grandkids. We see a lot of that shit up there in old Dover."

The new (or newly enforced) leash laws in Dover are most often directed at residents of old Dover like White, who had spent their whole life letting their dogs roam old Dover when the space was more open and less regulated.

Some of these conflicts over city ordinances flared up in the summer of 2017 around a mess in the yard of a resident of old Dover. That summer, the local paper ran a story under the headline "Dover Shop Project Draws Mayor's Ire," which outlined the escalating feud between Dover's new mayor and the grandson of a 93-year-old resident.[5] At the center of the kerfuffle was the Depression-era man's garage, which his grandson was cleaning for him. As the cleanup project stretched into its second week—with the contents of the garage piled in the driveway—the ongoing conflict between the mayor and the grandson over the mess became heated. In the paper, the mayor is described as "seething."[6] Online, people were incensed that the mayor had called the sheriff on the family. As the story became trending news, generating more and more comments and shares, readers lamented the changes in the broader community. Predictably, the new mayor was called a Californian (she's not, but neither is she from the area).

The more thoughtful of the online warriors suggested that, in the past, the mayor would have offered to help rather than called the sheriff. Twenty years earlier, regarding a similar situation, records show the city council dealing with another yard that was "starting to look real messy." Rather than calling the sheriff, however, the town leaders at the time decided to "talk to his mother and drop some hints." It was noted there was nothing in the ordinances that would make a messy yard against local codes.

In 2017, by contrast, the mayor called the sheriff to accompany her to the garage-cleaning project that was taking on a life of its own. When the officer told the mayor that a messy driveway did not violate any regulations and there was nothing to be done about the extended garage cleaning, the newspaper article reports that she threatened to enact new city regulations.[7]

City Ordinance 158 was adopted about a year later in a 3–1 vote. The City of Dover's new ordinance declared that no junk "shall be kept, accumulated, or stored within the public right-of-way, public property, or in the open on private property." The ordinance goes on to thoroughly define junk as including, but not limited to "manufactured goods, appliances, fixtures, scrap metal, salvaged building materials, agricultural or yard wastes, plastics, garbage, furniture, rags, clothing or accessories, paper, or paper products, glass, machinery or vehicle parts, inoperable or unlicensed vehicles, construction wastes, or any other personal property, whether of value or valueless, that is demolished, discarded, dismantled or partially dismantled, dilapidated, or deteriorated so it cannot be used for its original intended use."[8]

Reading over this list and then taking a look at my yard, I realize that, depending on who was looking at it, I could be cited. My ongoing gardening projects often include a pile of manure delivered by a friend with horses ("agricultural waste") and piles of cardboard and newspaper ("paper, or paper products") as I kill off different sections of the lawn for a new garden bed.

While most people in old Dover have beautiful, very tidy yards, and appreciate tidy yards, these kinds of ordinances essentially are designed to criminalize behaviors associated with the working class. For example, defining "junk" to include vehicle parts and inoperable vehicles "in the open on public property" makes it illegal to do vehicle repair in your own driveway. What gets designated as "personal property" that is "discarded" is largely up for interpretation. For intergenerational homes that may be filled with people, space becomes a premium and yards become prized play areas. At what point does a bike or playhouse or doll left outside become "junk"? These gray areas mean that the sheriff's office can get involved, issue citations, and levy fines. For people with disposable income, a lawyer can make those go away. But for the most part, working-class people don't have a lawyer on retainer and they may not have the money to pay a fine, meaning that the charges can escalate as they weave their way through the criminal justice system. One old-time resident in her eighties told me that she is afraid to hang clothes out to dry on a clothesline due to what she referred to as "the stipulations." While I didn't find any specific rule against clotheslines, "clothing" is included in the ordinance as junk. Her comments suggest the kind of anxieties residents of old Dover residents feel in the face of these new ordinances issued by newcomers.

These kinds of ordinances suggest the logical inconsistencies at work in this space. Old-time residents are told that the beloved beach they'd raised their children on is and was always "private property" and they have no rights to it. Yet, now that the development has been built, the city council can pass a new ordinance criminalizing garage cleaning on private property as it suits them.

Ted Foster's final, wistful statement about old Dover seems apt here: "There was a freedom which is gone now. It's all heavily regulated.

Regulated by people who don't want to comply with regulations." Perhaps what this quote misses, though, is that the people with money have the political and economic power to remake or skirt regulations to preserve their interests. Even if those interests are only a classed sense of what a yard should look like, these ordinances are about exerting power.

This power also extends to naming, as people in old Dover just hope that Dover stays Dover. A rumor has circulated claiming that, if folks from new Dover get enough seats on the city council, the name of the town will be changed to Mill Lake, the name of the development thus swallowing the little town whole. It seems unlikely that the name would be changed, but it's not out of the realm of possibilities. The junk ordinance notwithstanding, the current city administrators seem more concerned with keeping the sewer operating than delving into divisive issues. Still, it's easy to understand where the rumors and anxiety would come from. There are a million points of division between the old and new communities.

For now, though, the town is still Dover, split between the Mill Lake community and old Dover (or perhaps "historic Dover," a new, euphemistic moniker that may be gaining traction among the old-timers). The new buildings face away from the historic homes of old Dover, and even the streets bear witness to this division. As newcomer Amy Johns pointed out, when it snows, the easiest way to see where the development starts is to look at the roads. "There's a line in the road that is shoveled and not shoveled," she said. "The development plows; the city doesn't."

This division, however, did bring some unexpected forms of community cohesion, just not between new and "historic" Dover. For some of the residents who lived in old Dover but weren't necessarily "old-timers," the development finally meant that they were part of the old-timers' club. As Evan Johnson told me, "We used to be considered on the wrong side of the highway. There's the five or six houses over here on this side of the old highway there where the post office was here, and we were on the wrong side of the highway." Johnson had lived there for thirty years on "the wrong side of the highway" and people would tell him, "You guys aren't really a part of Dover." With Mill Lake in place, however, the boundaries have been redrawn. Johnson laughed as he assured me that "now we're part of old Dover."

CONCLUSION

Throughout my research, I had hoped to find some kind of documentation to verify the promises made (or not made) by the developers about what the new community would look like. Old Dover residents all told similar stories about those promises. They felt they had had assurances from Don Wilson and others that the new Dover would strive for a close-knit community as it once had been, with a public beach, a free boat launch, and maybe even a school that would keep Dover kids in Dover. Based on these assurances, these residents opted for change, hoping they could spare the city from simply becoming a bedroom community for Sandpoint. They wanted a community again, a place where neighbors gathered together, children roamed the streets, and everyone could enjoy the river.

I had hoped that the notes and tapes of the many discussions with the city council would allow me to parse out what promises had been made and what was simply wishful thinking on the part of old Dover residents. The blank tapes and missing notes, however, would ensure that those promises—if they existed—would remain elusive. We will probably never really know what promises were actually made—and thus will never know what promises were never kept.

However, with the development in place (and growing) and a community of newcomers forming in Mill Lake, it seems clear that promises made or promises broken are not the key factors fueling divisions between Mill Lake and "historic" Dover. The lack of a free boat launch continues to upset residents of old Dover, who now have to pay to launch their boats at the marina, but the developer also created a plethora of public spaces in an attempt to make the development inclusive and offer new amenities to all residents, old and new.

Even if there was a free boat launch, however, it seems unlikely that Dover would be less divided. A range of barriers all contribute to the continuing schism: deeply held cultural values around social class, the physical structures of the new development and its amenities, and different perspectives between old and new on what makes a vital community. Dover is cleaved by divergent sets of values, not by broken promises.

You see the results of these values everywhere across Dover. The old mayor, with his suspenders and hat, stepped down from serving the community after the development was built. He was replaced by one of Mill Lake Development's permanent residents—a woman with plenty of business know-how—who ran formal meetings in the beautiful city hall by the lake. Dogs abound in Dover, but now they are on leashes, being walked on miles of paved trails instead of roaming free alongside young people looking to have fun at the old mill site. Well-manicured lawns are maintained by retirees whose families live all over the county, while old-timers confront a future where they are the last of their families who will call Dover home.

For many people, however, these changes can be hard to articulate. Who is against walking trails and grassy lawns and a fancy city hall? The social class values of Mill Lake often do not sit right with the folks in old Dover, but naming that discomfort can be difficult, especially in a culture that venerates the values of the middle classes and the affluent. So instead, the residents of old Dover focus on promises they believe were broken, channeling their disillusionment into the idea that, had the developer just listened to them more and fulfilled his obligations to them, then the community would be stronger and more inclusive, and it might have captured the magic of old Dover in its glory days.

But the patterns of amenity migration and changes brought by "forever tourists" are simply not designed with community cohesion in mind. They are designed to maximize value for the developer. They are not systems intended to bridge the gap between rural, working-class populations and the more affluent populations that want to make some rural areas their new homes. Even a development such as Mill Lake—which did seem to try its best within the logic of amenity migration—is not intended to forge new kinds of community cohesion. Just as old Dover was never built with the stability of the community in mind (it was built to supply labor as long as labor was needed), Mill Lake was not built with the needs and desires of the working class in mind. With the mill gone and the value of the landscape tied to its role as a commodity, Mill Lake will always sit with its back to "historic" Dover, waiting for it to fade away.

Conclusion

Everything That's Old Is New Again

MILL LAKE IS a simulacrum for an American West that never existed. Mill Lake is old-timey streetlamps and fountains set against the scenic beauty of the river and the mountains. Mill Lake is a sparkling new Dover City Hall that sits at the lake's edge with vaulted ceilings and exposed beams, showing off timber that at one time would have been harvested by Dover residents and processed at the Dover mill (but today probably came from Canada). Mill Lake means realtors rushing around looking for the omnipresent moose to entice buyers with a "[Mill Lake] moment," hoping that the moose doesn't charge when they find it.

What is missing from this simulacrum, of course, are the people of old Dover, who, in small and large ways, are erased from the community. Each single change is magnified against the backdrop of historic changes. Today, in old Dover, a marooned 4-H bus sits in someone's yard. It is half storage unit and half garden statue, a reminder of a time when a small community could fill a bus with kids and head to a neighboring community equally full of kids. In Mill Lake, streets are named after the old-timers whose families settled Dover a hundred years ago but whose children cannot afford to live on the streets that bear them.

What happened in Dover is happening across the Pacific Northwest and the American West more broadly. Communities that undergo processes like this are sometimes referred to as "lucky," since the alternative in the American West is to be essentially erased off the map. The winners

C.1. A decorative fountain in Mill Lake and a walking trail that skirts it.

of these processes talk about rural revitalization, but the process is inherently uneven. Wealth only returns to areas that were previously exploited in a boom-and-bust cycle by people who accumulated wealth elsewhere. When wealth returns, it must extract the resources of the community again. Now, instead of clearing timber, workers clear tables and they fight to survive in an especially exploitive service economy, in which Idaho law in 2020 sets the minimum wage for tipped workers at $3.35 an hour.[1] For the residents of old Dover, this doesn't feel like revitalization.

But the processes and histories that brought Mill Lake to Dover (and other developments to other communities) are often hard to discern. They are obscured behind the notion that the "market" is a natural force, sweeping across the region in ways that cannot be altered. This often leads to anger from working-class people, but it is anger coupled with frustration and apathy. The folks of old Dover learned a long time ago that their rights as a community were never going to outweigh the prospect of

C.2. A bus that served the Bonner County 4-H Club sits marooned as both a decoration and storage unit in a Dover yard.

profits. They had gleaned stability and prosperity when their labor was key to making those profits, but now that landowners profited by marketing the scenic beauty of the landscape, there is no longer a place for them, and they have resigned themselves to this seeming "progress."

Sometimes this anger at the injustice of the system finds its way to "environmentalists," despite the evidence indicating that the timber companies, competing in a global market, themselves abandoned these communities in order to make more profit elsewhere. This anger is then amplified by those who claim that tourist-based economies are more environmentally sound than extractive industries, which is a debatable claim. But more importantly, such claims suggest that the human suffering of the people left behind is an acceptable price to pay to protect the natural world. It suggests that having a beautiful place to tootle around in a motorboat or ski is more important than people's ability to provide for their families.

Against these debates, it bears repeating that "the market" is not a natural force. The practices and policies that we loosely call "the free market" are anything but "free" and were created by the people who benefit from them, in order for their interests to *seem* natural. Across time and throughout history, most people have lived in arrangements that did *not* lead to the kinds of boom-and-bust cycles that have gripped the American West. And it is possible to create a future that does not rely on them.

"FIXING" THE SPACES OF THE WEST

Before one can imagine a different future, however, one must reckon with the realities of the past. What happened in Dover is not an aberration but rather the product of a capitalist system reorganizing its exploitation of human and natural resources.

As I have noted throughout this book, rural gentrification is a type of "spatial fix," as described by David Harvey, used to shore up capitalism's inherent contradictions. According to Harvey, the processes of capitalist accumulation are sustained in a series of expansionary patterns. First, capitalism functions by establishing a landscape in which workers and resources contribute to the accumulation of wealth for the elite. But the extraction of this wealth is always unsustainable under an economic system that requires constant growth. This instability requires the system be geographically expansive. In order to sustain itself, then, capitalism must seek out "spatial fixes," expanding into new spaces to find workers, resources, and landscapes to exploit. To increase profits, the timber industry looked abroad to where timber was cheaper to cut. And once the existing capitalist landscapes have been devalued, they become ripe for new organizations of labor and resources in the face of capitalism's destructive expansion.[2]

The expansion of white settlers into the American West functioned as the first "spatial fix" for US capitalism, seeking out new natural resources to sustain wealth and economic growth. Timber mills, like mines and agriculture, presented a massive opportunity for capitalist expansion. In *Capital*, Karl Marx argues that this process, what he calls "primitive accumulation," was the first and most necessary step in creating capitalism.

For capitalism to take a foothold as the dominant economic arrangement first in Europe and then in places it colonized, it required wealth to accelerate the process. This wealth came in the form of gold from "the New World" and cotton from India and ivory from Africa. Capitalism required that resources be pillaged from around the world to build wealth to start this economic arrangement.[3] A version of this process unfolded in the American West in the nineteenth and twentieth centuries, as the raw materials (timber, ore, agricultural products) of the landscape were extracted to create wealth, largely for corporations on the East Coast who used the "spatial fix" of western expansion to fuel their incessant need for economic growth.

But, just as in the case of Europe's accumulation of resources from "the New World," western expansion required laborers to process those raw materials (and make wages that would enable them to turn around and purchase the goods produced from those materials). Thus, as part of the project of manifest destiny, businesses and the US government worked to convince settlers to colonize Indigenous lands and "find prosperity." What made Weyerhaeuser and other timber barons wealthy was the labor of the people who cut and processed the trees, the labor of the mothers and fathers who raised the children who would go into the woods, the labor of farmers who produced the 8,000 calories a day that it took to keep them fed.

Industrialists needed white settlers to claim Indigenous land, but the intention was certainly not to make these masses of mostly new immigrants rich—it was to use them as an offensive line against Indigenous people and then to use their labor to extract the riches of the West for the benefits of the few. This process required a massive cultural project of dehumanization and violence against Indigenous peoples. As the scholar Dr. Philip Stevens notes in his discussion of artwork around Idaho highlighting the violence against Indigenous people by settlers, this art was created to normalize "the belief that these particular morals and beliefs are the only morals and beliefs. Everyone then becomes quickly assessed by a Eurocentric migrant standard and begins to fall into a hierarchy of identities."[4] As Stevens clarifies, "If the pursuit of happiness for your culture includes the individualized accumulation of wealth and resources, bereft of need for royal title or pedigree, then those who do not attempt to harvest as you do are not human or at least are less human. Perhaps a 'savage' is a better term."[5] This process of dehumanization naturalized capitalist accumulation on Indigenous land in the West (and of course, elsewhere).

Dover exists, then, because enormous tracts of the American West were wrenched away from Indigenous people and given to the railroad, which turned around and sold them to already rich men to build their fortunes, fortunes built on the back of men who often worked in desperate conditions. In North Idaho, the timber industry was created and controlled by very few, very wealthy families who used "individual accumulation" to create even more massive fortunes for themselves. This process was largely hidden behind an ideology that suggested to working people that they could live out the American dream if they would just put their backs into their work.

But capitalism as a system is unsustainable and inevitably destroys these spaces and labor practices by depleting natural resources and exploiting the bodies of laborers. Harvey argues that the only way for capitalism to survive is through boom-and-bust cycles in which the rich regain control of the wealth when economies and markets falter.[6] The laborers' long-term prosperity and sustainability, necessary for the accumulation of wealth, is not a goal of this system. In fact, the continual reorganization of capitalist practices necessitates the economic misfortune of workers as part of the devaluing of once-prosperous landscapes in order to create new opportunities for capitalism.

In other words, the corporations that built North Idaho—the lumber barons like Weyerhaeuser—didn't create it with a long-term vision in place. They saw timber extraction as a one-time activity. A 1901 newspaper editorial, for example, asks, "What will sustain our town after the commercial timber has been cut from our lands?" The editorial acknowledges that corporations never intended timber to be a long-term industry in the region. The plan was simply to cut what was easy to access and then to sell off the land.[7]

As timber continued to be profitable, especially after WWII, working families in the area assumed that this prosperity would be the norm. Once their labor became unnecessary or threatened to cut into corporate profits, however, capitalism as a system abandons that space for other spaces where profit is higher. At precisely the moment that mill workers were gaining financial security—primarily through strong unions—the mills began closing. North Idaho would continue to produce as much timber as it did in the 1980s right up until the housing crisis of 2008, but it was being done with far fewer workers and mills.[8] The mills in North Idaho still pumping out this lumber rely increasingly on automation. The mechanization that led to job loss in the timber industry was especially cruel to the working class, whose jobs were replaced by machines, and the timber corporations were happy to let environmental regulations take the blame. In the Pacific Northwest, railroad and timber barons used Indigenous land and immigrant bodies to create huge amounts of wealth, but when that wealth was threatened due to a globalizing timber economy, these communities were abandoned by the capitalist class.

Dover's struggles with water and sewage exemplify this abandonment. The moment the profitability of the mill declined, the mill owners abdicated any responsibility for continuing to provide safe, clean drinking water for the community whose labor had created so much wealth for timber companies. The town was left to rot. When the mill finally closed (and then burned down right before the mill owners might have had to reckon with EPA regulations regarding the old mill buildings), the citizens of Dover were left with no job opportunities, water they couldn't drink, and houses they couldn't sell. Then, after years of struggling with these infrastructure woes, the aging sewer system began to falter. Rather than working with the community to sell a small parcel of land at a reasonable market value to help Dover build a new sewer system, however, the same mill owners who abdicated responsibility for the drinking water refused to work with the town on the sewer system unless the community gave up their rights to zone the mill site according to the community's vision for its growth.

But the mill owners, doing business as Shamrock, were not held accountable—at all—for the failing water system or their successful attempts to force the city to rezone their property. Instead, using federal grants for low-income communities, as well as the time, energy, and taxes of the local people, Dover rebuilt its infrastructure. Shamrock then sold the land—now equipped with modern water and sewer systems and recently rezoned for a massive development—for millions to a new development company. Again, the suffering and labor of the locals were leveraged to create profits for a select few.

This destruction of old Dover—first as a space where the Kalispel people had lived for thousands of years and then as a space where working-class families could thrive—is not an accident or an aberration but rather a key means through which the capitalist class shores up its economic interests. The destruction of old Dover, both in terms of infrastructure and community cohesion, allowed the mill owners to rezone and sell the property as desirable real estate, dramatically increasing the price of the land. By making the mill site undesirable for manufacturing, a sizeable "rent gap," or the difference between "the potential ground rent" (what the mill site was worth as a development) "and the actual ground rent capitalized under the present land use" (what the land was worth as a failing mill), was created.[9] Thus, the rent gap produced profit in Harvey's "spatial fix" cycle of building, destroying, and rebuilding. In Dover, the mill owners reimagined the space through zoning and design to once again profit off the same land.

The crises of capitalism that necessitate the destruction of landscapes in order to generate profit through their rebuilding are about more than literal buildings and construction. These processes also build political and economic systems that shore up the ideologies and economic interests of those with power in these communities, thereby creating and legitimizing new organizations of wealth extraction from the land and the workers.

Just as Harvey outlines, then, the destruction and decay of a space like Dover, thanks to the exploitation of capitalism, created new "fixes," new opportunities for the landscape to become profitable after its devaluation. The systemic neglect of timber, mining, and other rural communities in the American West is not an unintended side effect of shifts in free-market capitalism but rather the predictable outcome of capitalist accumulation. Any temporary prosperity brought to those communities was a sort of side effect, and now their abandonment makes them vulnerable to new forms of exploitation: commodifying their natural beauty in order to sell access to nature at a premium. With these landscapes made undesirable because of such systematic neglect, the capitalist system can reorganize its operations. The "fix" here is to make the land cheaper for investors (yet still too expensive for economically depressed locals), allowing those with capital to buy and repackage it at an immense profit. The natural resources become scenic amenities for those who have accumulated wealth outside of the area. And environmental regulation, from this perspective, is not actually about the environment but about conserving spaces for consumption by amenity migrants.

This process—economic decline followed by development—often seems a "natural" consequence (and one that neglected communities are supposed to celebrate), but these changes are neither coincidences nor natural. They are systems designed to exploit the landscape and workers in new ways.

Yet in debates about the impacts of development, the histories of these systems are often ignored. The groundwork for rural development was laid over a hundred years ago, when land occupied by Indigenous people was given to massive corporations that enlisted white settlers in a vast project of infrastructure development requiring systemic racial violence. These events would establish economic systems, laws, policies, and cultural attitudes that still deeply inform the American West today. Whether we acknowledge this legacy or not, these histories underwrite our contemporary discussions of rural development, as evidenced in a place like Dover.

And the wealth stemming from these histories is still at play in today's economy. Today, the Weyerhaeuser Company owns millions of acres from Canada to Latin America and from Asia to Australia, making it one of the largest owners of timberland in the world. In 2010, the company "transitioned" to a real estate investment trust (REIT) because that structure created a "tax efficiency" that allowed it "to increase [its] timberland earnings" by avoiding federal income taxes.[10]

A DIFFERENT DOVER

Places like Dover are considered the winners in this changing landscape, giving us insight into what rural communities have been asked to accept. When any kind of economic growth is made to seem impossible to imagine, and when economic booms and busts have simply become a feature of contemporary life, being targeted for development in the rural West can sometimes feel like a victory.

But it is worth asking if rural communities should accept this as normal. Perhaps development should serve communities, not the other way around.

I have spent a lot of time imagining a different Dover, one that invited new people to join the community but that also offered real opportunities to the existing residents in return. I return to Erik Loomis's belief that "when environmentalism remains primarily about improving people's lives, there is a seat at the center of the table for the representatives of working-class Americans. Only when we narrow environmentalism down to the protections of space of human activity does that go away."[11] So what could development look like in the rural West when you place the dignity of people's lives and the autonomy of local communities at the center of the conversation?

Unfortunately, because of the legal and economic systems in place in the United States (informed by the histories discussed above), there are not many examples of what such a world might look like. But one might be the Bells Bend community outside of Nashville, Tennessee. In 2008, locals in the small community stopped a $4 billion (yes, billion) development called "May Town" that would have brought stores, apartments, and office space to the pastoral farmlands. The community launched a massive public relations campaign against the development and, with help from allies in Nashville who worried that May Town would have drained the life from the city's downtown, halted it.[12]

Not content with simply stopping the development, however, Bells Bend decided that it would build its own vision of economic growth for the community. It worked to make the area a haven for small organic farms with community markets and "businesses that cater to kayaking, hiking, caving, birding, camping, biking or whatever else crunchy granola people like to do," according to one local reporter.[13] People in Bells Bend attempted to envision a model of growth that kept the "rural" in rural development and tried to meet the needs of the existing population, not simply woo outsiders with more wealth.[14]

When I envision a different Dover, then, I start at the end of the road, where the old barn sits. A barn was essential for a mill operation before machinery came along—it housed the horses that provided the power. Even today, the old barn in Dover sits, as it has for a century, surrounded by open fields that once grew hay to feed the horses.

Today it is part of Mill Lake Development's holdings. It has been christened "the Homestead Barn" and renovated as an event center with "graceful arched ceilings, highlighted by the soft glow of chandeliers and twinkling string lights," as described on the development's website. Most weekends in the summer, there is a wedding or another event there.

For Dover resident John White, the traffic speeding down the road to the barn is a giveaway as to whom the barn serves. "They're driving around in BMWs or Mercedes-Benz," he said. "What we have down there are spoiled rich kids." He lamented that there was no police presence on this road, because after a function at the barn, "they come haul ass through the neighborhoods . . . They come out of there drunk, and they're just hauling ass. It's just a matter [of time] before somebody gets hit."

But imagine a Dover where a portion of the mill site was zoned for agricultural use and the old barn housed animals again. The land around the barn could have been set aside for agriculture and put under a long-term lease to local farmers. Such an operation could run a small market serving the community, where locals could walk their dog down the road and grab a dozen eggs or cheese or a few tomatoes in the late summer for dinner.

Maybe this farm would be successful enough that, in cooperation with the community, it could host a pumpkin patch in the fall or a fiber arts fair in the summer. And if these events and the community market brought in people from Sandpoint or other area towns, maybe someone would open a diner in the long-shuttered saddle repair shop in old Dover using food grown at "the Old Barn Farm." Maybe the children and grandchildren of the residents of old Dover would find a spot to sell furniture made from driftwood to the folks who come to town for the diner. Businesses might pop up—at first out of people's garages—renting bikes to ride on trails along the river or giving horseback tours of the bluff. And more visitors would come if the town opened "Dover Beach Park," ensuring public access to one of the last sandy beaches on the increasingly developed lake.

Perhaps the land along the old mill road could be zoned residential, and working families could afford to buy a modest house there. The streets that got built would open into old Dover. The new and old homes would sit face to face, and grandchildren would build homes next door to their grandparents. It would be a place where the city council could write a junk ordinance that forced the mill owners to clean up the mess they left behind and to restore the wetlands. It would be a place where Shamrock either provided clean drinking water to the community or handed over its land as compensation. It would be a world where people would end up in prison for poisoning a community with contaminated water for years. It would be a place where the city would have spent its time applying for grants to build trails to explore the beaches and wetlands. To be fair, it would also probably be a place where teenagers should not be shooting each other with BB guns for entertainment. But it would also be a place without a marina; without worries about the riverbank eroding, it would be a Dover without riprap. It would be a Dover where you could launch your boat for free and fish on the river. It would be a place where sandy beaches and a bluff covered in wildflowers were for the community. It would be a Dover built on the belief that environmentalism must center all people—across races and classes—to preserve the natural world for everyone, not just for those who can write a check for their piece of paradise.

LOSING PLACES

As I write these words about a Dover that might have been, it is clear that much of this book is about loss, about losing meaningful places from the past and losing a future that might have been. For many residents of old Dover, this loss was made visceral when the developers dynamited the bluff. One longtime Dover resident shared the emotion of watching this beloved space altered: "It was really sad when they blew up the rock [on the bluff] to put the road in. I was coming across the Long Bridge . . . I didn't hear anything, but out of the corner of my eye, I see this big cloud go up. It was literally like they dropped a bomb on it. They set it all off at once." Even for the residents of Dover who had resigned themselves to the development, seeing the changes and portions of the bluff reduced to rubble brought home the profound sadness of change.

I also brought my own sense of loss to Dover and to this project. I arrived in Dover in the 1990s, a child who'd been set adrift because of the farm crisis of the 1980s. We were forced off the ranch, the place where my grandpa (and later grandma) were buried. The loss of place is something that feels acutely painful to me. I watched how that loss shaped me and seemed to break some of the people it touched.

Many years later, I read that on another ranch close to ours, the 12,000-year-old remains of a toddler were unearthed, a controversial DNA test establishing that the child was a "direct ancestor [to] many of today's native people in the Americas."[15] I tried to imagine my attachment to my family's ranch extended to 12,000 years, to hundreds of generations, and then imagine the traumatic losses felt by Indigenous peoples.

Dr. Philip Stevens asks settlers to reorient their perspective by imagining the connections between place and identity for Indigenous peoples: "If your culture and identity are situated in a particular place for many generations, then your culture and identity will create a strong connection with that place."[16] By contrast, settlers in places like Idaho in the American West have brought with them a belief in the mutability of space and identity: "It seems that they have a particular cultural perspective that allows them to view place as interchangeable. In essence, place is a mutable thing: lush green lawns in the desert, New York, New Hampshire. Of course, like the myriad of switches and dials on a sound-mixing table, people have their own level of each switch that cumulatively forms their overall identity, which can create blurred boundaries.[17]

This mutability leads to places like Mill Lake, which, like the mill before it, attempts to transform the place where the river meets the lake into a place for further settlement. Dial back the working-class laborers and mastery of the natural world, dial up the comfortable amenities and scenic beauty.

But the losses felt by the old-timer residents in the face of this mutability, like my own sense of loss for my family's ranch, are dwarfed by the profound losses of Indigenous communities. As I was writing about the loss of the beach to the people of Dover, the heartache of Francis Cullooyah stayed with me: "How things would be so good if I was able to walk on the shores of Lake Pend Oreille today and say 'this is mine.' I still say 'this is mine,' but I'm only kidding myself. We have places we just can't go anymore."[18]

Likewise, Shirley Seth, a member of the Kalispel tribe, shared her thoughts: "I think of having land, even partial pieces of our aboriginal boundaries where the Kalispel used to be free to come and go, I think that would be totally amazing." She continued, "It would be overwhelming for some of my people . . . to say we got some of this back. I think it would be a miracle almost."[19]

In 2017, members of the Kalispel tribe traveled from Sandpoint to their reservation in Usk, Washington, in handmade sturgeon-nosed and dugout canoes. That fifty-mile trip downriver marked the first time tribal members had made the journey in nearly a hundred years.[20] Acknowledging the power of that act in the face of such tremendous losses, I sometimes let myself think about a Dover where the mill owners gave the land back to the Kalispel people. I imagine a Dover where the Kalispel people launch their canoes from the beach.

It is my belief that until we reckon with the histories of oppression that have impacted both Indigenous people and the working-class peoples who displaced them, these alternate futures will remain elusive. Unless we understand the dynamics of the past and the ways our economy structures our present, communities will find it next to impossible to imagine paths forward that center our real human needs.

NOTES

1 Kinnaird, "[Mill Lake] Decision Inspires Both Delight and Horror."
2 Phillips, "Counterurbanisation and Rural Gentrification."
3 Pilgeram, "'How Much Does Property Cost Up There?'"
4 Harris and Tarchak, "Small-Town America Is Dying."
5 Kusmin, "Rural America at a Glance."
6 Gosnell and Abrams, "Amenity Migration," 303.
7 McCarthy, "Rural Geography," 130.
8 Hines, "In Pursuit of Experience"; Ghose, "Big Sky or Big Sprawl?"
9 Ghose, "Big Sky or Big Sprawl?," 530.
10 Ghose, "Big Sky or Big Sprawl?," 529.
11 Hines, "In Pursuit of Experience"; Ghose, "Big Sky or Big Sprawl?"; Nelson and Nelson, "Global Rural."
12 Hines, "In Pursuit of Experience," 285.
13 Ward, "Chronic Poverty, Community Decline, and Amenity-Rich Growth," 171.
14 Cloke and Little, *The Rural State?*, 18.
15 Abrams et al., "Re-Creating the Rural, Reconstructing Nature," 278.
16 Gosnell and Abrams, "Amenity Migration"; Hines, "Post-Industrial Regime of Production/Consumption"; Pilgeram, "'How Much Does Property Cost Up There?'"
17 Robbins et al., "Writing the New West," 375.
18 Harvey, "Globalization and the 'Spatial Fix,'" 25; Nelson, Trautman, and Nelson, "Latino Immigrants and Rural Gentrification"; Pilgeram, "'How Much Does Property Cost Up There?'"
19 Harvey, "Globalization and the 'Spatial Fix,'" 25.
20 Harvey, "Globalization and the 'Spatial Fix,'" 25.
21 Harvey, "Globalization and the 'Spatial Fix.'"
22 Harvey, "Globalization and the 'Spatial Fix.'"

1   Kalispel Tribe of Indians, "Culture: A River and a People," Kalispel Tribe of Indians (website), accessed November 2019, www.kalispeltribe.com/our-tribe /land-culture.

2   Harvey, "Globalization and the 'Spatial Fix,'" 25.

3   Reed Lewis (research geologist, Idaho Geological Survey), personal interview with the author, October 25, 2016.

4   "Ice Age Floods, Study of Alternatives, Section D—Background."

5   Salish Culture Committee, "Salish Creation Story" (from the Confederation of Salish and Kootenai Tribes, 2004), The Salish Tribe (website), by Sarah Devlin, accessed November 2019, https://salishtribe.wordpress.com/salish -culture/the-salish-creation-story.

6   Hodges and Gillis, "Archaeological Investigations at 10-BR-14."

7   Weaver, Bard, and Warner, *Other Side of Sandpoint*.

8   Lyons, "Recognizing the Archaeological Signatures of Resident Fisheries."

9   Kevin Lyons (cultural resource manager, Kalispel Tribe), personal interview with the author, March 17, 2017.

10 Hodges and Gillis, "Archaeological Investigations at 10-BR-14"; Weaver, Bard, and Warner, *Other Side of Sandpoint*.

11 Nisbet, "'A Place to Build a House On."

12 Weaver, Bard, and Warner, *Other Side of Sandpoint*, 41.

13 Weaver, Bard, and Warner, *Other Side of Sandpoint*, 44.

14 Lyons, personal interview.

15 Weaver, Bard, and Warner, *Other Side of Sandpoint*, 45.

16 Renk, *Glorious Field for Sawmills*, 1.

17 Renk, *Glorious Field for Sawmills*.

18 Holstine, "Cabinet Landing," 25. Pages 9–29 detail the construction of the Northern Pacific Railroad.

19 Nokes, *Massacred for Gold*.

20 Faiman-Silva, "Tribal Land to Private Land," 193.

21 Peterson, "Some Colonization Projects."

22 Northern Pacific Railroad Company, *Vast Areas of the Best Wheat Lands!*, 18.

23 Kammer, "Land and Law in the Age of Enterprise" 191.

24 Kammer, "Land and Law in the Age of Enterprise," 195.

25 Kammer, "Land and Law in the Age of Enterprise," 192.

26 Renk, *Glorious Field for Sawmills*, 19.

27 Sears, Roebuck and Co., *1897 Sears Roebuck Catalogue*.

28 Malone and Etulain, *American West*.

29 Renk, *Glorious Field for Sawmills*

30 "New Planer at the Dover Mill Starts Up," *Pend d'Oreille Review*, August 14, 1907.

31 Renk, *Glorious Field for Sawmills*, 77.

32 "I.W.W Defense Starts," *Pend d'Oreille Review*, January 30, 1920.

33 Renk, *Glorious Field for Sawmills*, 77.
34 Renk, *Glorious Field for Sawmills*, 87.
35 Renk, *Glorious Field for Sawmills*, 18.
36 "Portland Company," *Pend d'Oreille Review*, November 7, 1929.
37 Lyons, personal interview.
38 Fritz, "Land of the Kalispel."
39 *Kootenai County Republican*.
40 "Lumber Company," *Northern Idaho News*, May 19, 1944.
41 "Interior Designers Enthusiastic," *Sandpoint News Bulletin*, August 7, 1955.
42 Malone and Etulain, *American West*, 246.
43 Malone and Etulain, *American West*, 246.

CHAPTER 2: WATER, WATER EVERYWHERE

1 Smith, "Toward a Theory of Gentrification."
2 Darling, "City in the Country."
3 Nelson and Hines, "Rural Gentrification and Networks of Capital Accumulation."
4 Simmons et al., "Idaho's Forest Products Industry," 27.
5 Richardson, "Out on a Limb."
6 Deavers, "1980s a Decade of Broad Rural Stress."
7 Simmons et al., "Idaho's Forest Products Industry," 27.
8 Power, "Public Timber Supply," 345.
9 Simmons et al., "Idaho's Forest Products Industry," 8.
10 Power, "Public Timber Supply" 345.
11 Hagadone, "NAFTA and Idaho."
12 Quoted in Hagadone, "NAFTA and Idaho."
13 Jeff Faux, "NAFTA's Impact on U.S. Workers," *Working Economics Blog*, Economic Policy Institute, December 9, 2013, www.epi.org/blog/naftas-impact-workers.
14 Wear and Murray, "Federal Timber Restrictions."
15 Hardy Lyons (attorney at law representing Pack River Co.), "Letter to F. Warrer," 1973, archival data, accessed 2016.
16 Nelson, "Dover Seeks End to Water System Woes."
17 Lyons, "Letter to F. Warrer."
18 "New Water Tank," *Sandpoint News Bulletin*, May 11, 1951.
19 Kyle C. Bates (land manager, Shamrock Investment Company), "Letter to J. Weisz," March 26, 1984, archival data, accessed 2016.
20 Bates, "Letter to J. Weisz."
21 Bates, "Letter to J. Weisz."
22 "New Water Tank," *Sandpoint News Bulletin*, July 21, 1950.
23 Nelson, "Dover Seeks End to Water System Woes."
24 Nelson, "Dover Seeks End to Water System Woes."

25 "Dover's Water Grant Money," *Bonner County Daily Bee*, December 22, 1989.

26 "Dover Water on—for Now," *North Idaho News Network*, January 3, 1991.

27 Keating, "Dover, Idaho, Has Difficulty Keeping Water Pump Going."

28 Nelson, "Dover Seeks End to Water System Woes."

29 "Dover's Water Grant Money," *Bonner County Daily Bee*, December 22, 1989.

30 "Dover Grant Turned Down," *Bonner County Daily Bee*, December 21, 1988.

31 Buley, "Dover's 'Boil Water' Order."

32 Keating, "Dover, Idaho, Has Difficulty Keeping Water Pump Going."

33 Buley, "Dover Dry after Water Pump Breaks."

34 Buley, "Dover Dry after Water Pump Breaks."

35 George Hansen (chief operating officer, Shamrock Investment Company), "Letter to Users of the Dover Water System," December 14, 1990, archival data, accessed 2016.

36 "Dover Water on—for Now," *North Idaho News Network*, January 3, 1991.

37 Shamrock Investment Company, "Letter to Residents of Dover," December 11, 1991, archival data, accessed 2016.

38 Gunter, "Mill Leaves Mark on Dover Community."

39 Gunter, "Dover Mill Dismantling Raises Questions."

40 Gunter, "Dover Mill Dismantling Raises Questions."

41 Gunter, "Dover Mill Dismantling Raises Questions."

42 Keating, "Fire Destroys Abandoned Mill,"

43 Keating, "Fire Destroys Abandoned Mill."

44 McLean, "Firefighters Visit Mill Twice after Fire."

45 McLean, "Cause of Fire at Dover Mill Identified."

46 McLean, "Blaze Ravages Dover Mill."

CHAPTER 3: SHIT ROLLS DOWNHILL

1 Harvey, "Globalization and the 'Spatial Fix,'" 25.

2 Lawton, "Taking a Look Back at the 1980s Farm Crisis and Its Impacts," Farm Progress (website), August 22, 2016, www.farmprogress.com/marketing/taking-look-back-1980s-farm-crisis-and-its-impacts.

3 "Bombs Rock Idaho City Torn by Strife," *New York Times*, September 30, 1986.

4 Keating, "Many Ex-California Cops Retire to Idaho."

5 By the early 1990s, Shamrock Investment Company was most often doing business as "Dover Development."

6 City of Dover Archives. Notes from the Dover City Council Meeting, August 1, 1996.

7 Despite the help of the ever-patient Dover city clerk, who appeared to be as curious as I was to find the documents listed in the notes, those records could not be located, either because they were never entered into the public record or because they were lost.

8 City of Dover Archives. Notes from the Dover City Council Meeting, August 1, 1996.

9 City of Dover Archives. Notes from the Dover City Council Meeting, August 1, 1996.

10 Lobsinger, "City Debates Extending Services."

11 Lobsinger, "City Debates Extending Services."

12 Lobsinger, "Rocky Point Gains City Ear."

13 Lobsinger, "Rocky Point Gains City Ear."

14 Lobsinger, "Dover Leaning toward Sewer District Takeover."

15 Lobsinger, "Dover May Finalize Sewer Acquisition."

16 Lobsinger, "Dover Leaning toward Sewer District Takeover."

17 Rocky Point Sewer District Board, "Letter to P. o. R. P. S. District Concerning Proposed Wastewater Treatment System," September 15, 1995, archival data, accessed 2016.

18 William Herrington, "Letter to L. Dover Enterprises Concerning Acquisition of Property by the City of Dover," June 14, 1996, City of Dover Archives, accessed 2016.

19 Marty Jones, "Response to Letter Dated November 8, 1996" [to John F. Magnuson], November 26, 1996. City of Dover Archives, accessed 2016.

20 "Dover Mayor Letter to F. Elsaesser, Draft: Response to Letter Dated August 6, 1996," September 5, 1996, City of Dover Archives, accessed 2016.

21 City of Dover Archives. Public Hearing, September 24, 1996.

22 Turner, "Dover Residents Wary of Land Development."

23 William Herrington, "Letter to F. Elsaesser Concerning City of Dover v. Dover Enterprises Lp.," October 14, 1996, City of Dover Archives, accessed 2016.

24 "Dover Mayor Letter to A. a. L. John F. Magnuson, Response to Letter Dated November 8, 1996," November 26, 1996, City of Dover Archives, accessed 2016.

25 John F. Magnuson, Attorney at Law, "Letter to W. Herrington Concerning City of Dover v. Dover Enterprises, Lp.," December 13, 1996, City of Dover Archives, accessed 2016.

26 *City of Dover v. Dover Enterprises.*

27 "City of Dover Public Hearing Notice," *Bonner County Daily Bee*, March 4, 1997; "City of Dover Public Hearing Notice," *Bonner County Daily Bee*, April 5, 1997.

CHAPTER 4: IT'S ~~NOT~~ OVER IN DOVER

1 Turner, "Judge Rules for City."

2 Forest, "Huge [Mill Lake] Re-Development Project."

3 Kinnaird, "Waters Still Choppy."

4 Interestingly, those who worked to stop the development never brought up a stipulation from the 1997 court decision stating that, if Shamrock sold the land less than ten years after the agreement, then the city did not have to abide by

the zoning changes. It is unclear if anyone knew or remembered that particular part of the agreement.

5 Petersen, "It's Not Over in Dover."
6 Kinnaird, "[Mill Lake] Decision Inspires Both Delight and Horror."
7 Kinnaird, "Dover OKs Development."
8 "Construction Deed of Trust."

CHAPTER 5: ANARCHISTS ON THE BEACH

1 See, for example, Arlee Russell Hochschild's exploration of this debate in Louisiana in *Strangers in Their Own Land*.
2 Harvey, *Seventeen Contradictions*, 75.
3 Mackenzie, "Development Hurts Dover, Community."
4 Petersen, "[Mill Lake] Plan Not in City's Best Interests."
5 Hochschild, *Strangers in Their Own Land*, 74.
6 Hochschild, *Strangers in Their Own Land*, 258–59.
7 Pullum, "Beach Closure Angers Residents."
8 Yaw, "New More Facts."
9 Dover Beach Use Survey. Private archive, Dover, ID.
10 Kirkpatrick, "Pack River Explains Position on Property and Dover Beach."
11 Nichols, "Dover Beach: Commissioners Suggest Means to End Conflict."
12 Quoted in Nichols, "Dover Beach."
13 "Dover Residents Discuss Closure of Beach with County Commissioners," *Bonner County Daily Bee*, July 27, 1978.
14 Kinnaird, "Dover Probes Ways to Preserve Beach Access."
15 Stewart, "Dover Beach Feud Ongoing."
16 Neiwert, "Dover Beach: Who Really Owns It? Is the Question."

CHAPTER 6: A MILL LAKE MOMENT

1 Weber, "Three American Wests."
2 Harvey, "Globalization and the 'Spatial Fix.'"
3 Hunter, Boardman, and Saint Onge, "Association between Natural Amenities," 452.
4 McCarthy, "Rural Geography," 130.
5 Winkler et al., "Social Landscapes."
6 Winkler et al., "Social Landscapes," 479.
7 Winkler et al., "Social Landscapes," 479.
8 Weber, "Three American Wests." As Weber notes, there are also other types of land that comprise "the protected West," for example, military bases and Indian reservations.
9 In North Idaho, that system wasn't totally complete until 1991, when the residents of Wallace, Idaho, got most of their town listed on the National Register

of Historic Places and thus forced the federal government to build a freeway bypass around their downtown district, saving their town from being razed to make room for the freeway and eliminating the only stoplight on I-90 between Seattle and Boston.

10 "U.S. Federal Endangered and Threatened Species by Calendar Year." US Fish and Wildlife Service Environmental Conservation Online System, accessed November 2019, https://ecos.fws.gov/ecpo/reports/species-listings-count-by-year-report.

11 Malone and Etulain, *American West*, 285.

12 Of course, the rules of common sense did not necessarily apply to the clearing of forests, which used a logic that prioritized immediate profit over the long-term viability of the forest and ultimately of the timber industry in this region. For more information, see Loomis, *Empire of Timber*.

13 Kinnaird, "Waters Still Choppy."

14 Vukomanovic, "Exurbia as Physical and Social Space."

15 Hodges and Gillis, "Archaeological Investigations at 10-BR-14." See also Bard, Betts, and Lahren Jr., *Other Side of Sandpoint*.

16 Loomis, *Empire of Timber*.

17 Loomis, *Empire of Timber*, 213.

18 Loomis, *Empire of Timber*, 213.

19 Loomis, *Empire of Timber*, 212.

20 Clendenning, Field, and Kapp, "Comparison of Seasonal Homeowners and Permanent Residents."

21 Lorah and Southwick, "Environmental Protection," 258.

CHAPTER 7: A TALE OF TWO DOVERS

1 Or did the developer have a good sense of what the city council was likely to approve based on what they had already turned down?

2 Bonner County Treasurer's Office, "Tax Master Inquiry," email correspondence, November 18, 2019.

3 Sutherland, "Return of the Gentleman Farmer?"

4 Dover Restaurant Manager, "Re: Servers," email correspondence concerning Craigslist ad for servers, July 22, 2019.

5 Kinnaird, "Dover Shop Project Draws Mayor's Ire."

6 Kinnaird, "Dover Shop Project Draws Mayor's Ire."

7 Kinnaird, "Dover Shop Project Draws Mayor's Ire."

8 City of Dover, "Amendment to Chapter 6."

CONCLUSION. EVERYTHING THAT'S OLD IS NEW AGAIN

1 Idaho Department of Labor, "Frequently Asked Questions on Labor Laws."

2 Harvey, "Globalization and the 'Spatial Fix.'"

3 Marx, *Capital*, 873–76.

4 Stevens, "We Hold These Truths to Be Self-Evident," 159.

5 Stevens, "We Hold These Truths to Be Self-Evident," 159.

6 Harvey, "Globalization and the 'Spatial Fix.'"

7 Editorial, *Kootenai County Republican*, October 25, 1901.

8 Simmons et al., "Idaho's Forest Products Industry," 27.

9 Smith, "Toward a Theory of Gentrification."

10 "Weyerhaeuser Declares Special Dividend," *Weyerhaeuser News Room*, July 11, 2010.

11 Loomis, *Empire of Timber*, 237–38.

12 Woods, "Triumph of the Crunchy Granola People."

13 Woods, "Triumph of the Crunchy Granola People."

14 Nathan, "The Bend."

15 "Prehistoric Remains Reveal Roots of American Indians," WBUR (website), February 26, 2014, www.wbur.org/hereandnow/2014/02/26/montana-native -genome.

16 Stevens, "We Hold These Truths to Be Self-Evident," 159.

17 Stevens, "We Hold These Truths to Be Self-Evident," 159.

18 Quoted in Fritz, "Land of the Kalispel."

19 Quoted in Fritz, "Land of the Kalispel."

20 Botkin, "Kalispel Paddle the Pend Oreille."

BIBLIOGRAPHY

Abrams, Jesse B., Hannah Gosnell, Nicholas J. Gill, and Peter J. Klepeis. "Re-Creating the Rural, Reconstructing Nature: An International Literature Review of the Environmental Implications of Amenity Migration." *Conservation and Society* 10, no. 3 (2012): 270–84.

Bard, James C., Robert C. Betts and Sylvester L. Lahren Jr. "The Other Side of Sandpoint—Early History and Archaeology Beside the Track: The Sandpoint Archaeology Project 2006-2013." 2014. Prepared for the Idaho Transportation Department, District 1.

Bonner County Daily Bee. "City of Dover Public Hearing Notice." March 4, 1997.

———. "City of Dover Public Hearing Notice: Planned Unit Development Ordinance." April 5, 1997.

———. "Dover Grant Turned Down." December 21, 1988.

———. "Dover Residents Discuss Closure of Beach with County Commissioners." July 27, 1978.

———. "Dover's Water Grant Money Is a Swig of History." December 22, 1989.

Botkin, Katie. "Kalispel Paddle the Pend Oreille in Dugout Canoes, Embracing Historic Ties to the Waterway." *Spokesman-Review*, August 6, 2017.

Buley, Bill. "Dover Dry after Water Pump Breaks." *Bonner County Daily Bee*, October 18, 1990.

———. "Dover's 'Boil Water' Order to End Next Fall." *Bonner County Daily Bee*, December 21, 1989.

City of Dover. "Amendment to Chapter 6, Standards of All Zone Districts, & Definitions—Nuisances, Ordinance no. 158." https://cityofdover.id.gov/public-documents/city-dover-ordinances/.

City of Dover Archives. Notes from the Dover City Council Meeting. August 1, 1996.

———. Public Hearing. September 24, 1996.

City of Dover v. Dover Enterprises. CV-96-00943 (First Judicial District of the State of Idaho, December 24, 1996).

Clendenning, Greg, Donald R. Field, and Kirsten J. Kapp. "A Comparison of Seasonal Homeowners and Permanent Residents on their Attitudes toward Wildlife Management on Public Lands." *Human Dimensions of Wildlife* 10, no. 1 (2005): 3–17.

Cloke, Paul, and Jo Little. *The Rural State? Limits to Planning in Rural Society.* Oxford: Oxford University Press, 1990.

"Construction Deed of Trust." Bonner County Public Records. Filed July 14, 2004. https://erecorder.bonnercountyid.gov/bonnerweb/search/DOCSEARCH98S5?do cId=searchRowDOCCLAND-615873.

Darling, Eliza, "The City in the Country: Wilderness Gentrification and the Rent Gap." *Environment and Planning* A 37, no. 6 (2005): 1015–32.

Deavers, Kenneth L. "1980s a Decade of Broad Rural Stress." *Rural Development Perspectives* 7, no. 3 (1991): 2–5.

Faiman-Silva, Sandra L. "Tribal Land to Private Land: A Century of Oklahoma Choctaw Timberland Alienation from the 1880s to the 1980s." *Journal of Forest History* 32, no. 4 (October 1988): 191–204.

Forest, Jody. "Huge [Mill Lake] Re-Development Project Moves Forward." *The River Journal*, December 2003.

Fritz, Jane. "Land of the Kalispel." *Sandpoint Magazine* (Summer 1997). www.sand pointonline.com/sandpointmag/sms97/kalispel.html.

Ghose, Rina. "Big Sky or Big Sprawl? Rural Gentrification and the Changing Cultural Landscape of Missoula, Montana." *Urban Geography* 25, no. 6 (2004): 528–49.

Gosnell, Hannah, and Jesse Abrams. "Amenity Migration: Diverse Conceptualizations of Drivers, Socioeconomic Dimensions, and Emerging Challenges." *GeoJournal* 76, no. 4 (2011): 303–22.

Gunter, David. "Dover Mill Dismantling Raises Questions: Fate of Buildings, Hazmat Are Cause of Concern." *Bonner County Daily Bee*, April 22, 1992.

———. "Mill Leaves Mark on Dover Community." *Bonner County Daily Bee*, April 22, 1992.

Hagadone, Zach. "NAFTA and Idaho: Winners and Losers." *Sandpoint Reader*, November 4, 2016. https://sandpointreader.com/nafta-idaho-winners-losers.

Harris, Rachel L., and Lisa Tarchak. "Small-Town America Is Dying. How Can We Save It?" *New York Times*, December 22, 2018.

Harvey, David. "Globalization and the 'Spatial Fix.'" *Geographische Revue* 2 (2001): 23–30.

———. *Seventeen Contradictions and the End of Capitalism*. Oxford: Oxford University Press, 2014.

Hines, J. Dwight. "In Pursuit of Experience: The Postindustrial Gentrification of the Rural American West." *Ethnography* 11, no. 2 (2010): 285–308.

———. "The Post-Industrial Regime of Production/Consumption and the Rural Gentrification of the New West Archipelago." *Antipode* 44, no. 1 (2012): 74–97.

Hochschild, Arlie Russell. *Strangers in Their Own Land: Anger and Mourning on the American Right*. New York: The New Press, 2018.

Hodges, Charles M., and Nichole A. Gillis, Northwest Archaeological Associates, Inc. "Archaeological Investigations at 10-BR-14, [Mill Lake] Cut Bank Stabilization Project Bonner County, Idaho." 2007. Access granted by Idaho State Historical Society, State Historical Preservation Office.

Holstine, Craig. "Cabinet Landing and the Northern Pacific Railroad: Historical Perspectives." In *Archaeological Investigations at the Cabinet Landing Site (10BR413)*,

Bonner County, Idaho, edited by Keith Landreth, Keo Boreson, and Mary Condon, 9–40. Eastern Washington University Reports in Archaeology and History, Report Number 100-45. Cheney, WA: Archaeological and Historical Services, 1985.

Hunter, Lori, Jason D. Boardman, and Jarron M. Saint Onge. "The Association between Natural Amenities, Rural Population Growth, and Long-Term Residents' Economic Well-Being." *Rural Sociology* 70, no. 4 (2005): 452–69.

"Ice Age Floods, Study of Alternatives, Section D—Background." In *Ice Age Floods: Study of Alternatives and Environmental Assessment.* National Park Service, 2001. www.nps.gov/iceagefloods/d.htm.

Idaho Department of Labor. "Frequently Asked Questions on Labor Laws." Accessed August 2020. www.labor.idaho.gov/dnn/Businesses/Idaho-Labor-Laws/Labor -Laws-FAQ.

Kammer, Sean M. "Land and Law in the Age of Enterprise: A Legal History of Railroad Land Grants in the Pacific Northwest, 1864–1916." PhD diss., University of Nebraska, 2015.

Keating, Kevin. "Dover, Idaho, Has Difficulty Keeping Water Pump Going." *Spokesman-Review*, October 19, 1990.

———. "Fire Destroys Abandoned Mill, Imperils Homes." *Spokesman-Review*, May 9, 1992.

———. "Many Ex-California Cops Retire to Idaho." *Spokesman-Review*, January 27, 1995.

Kinnaird, Keith. "Dover OKs Development." *Bonner County Daily Bee*, September 4, 2004.

———. "Dover Probes Ways to Preserve Beach Access." *Bonner County Daily Bee*, September 25, 1998.

———. "Dover Shop Project Draws Mayor's Ire." *Bonner County Daily Bee*, August 5, 2017.

———. "[Mill Lake] Decision Inspires Both Delight and Horror." *Bonner County Daily Bee*, September 4, 2004.

———. "Waters Still Choppy for [Mill Lake] Marina Project." *Bonner County Daily Bee*, January 7, 1997.

Kirkpatrick, Rusty. "Pack River Explains Position on Property and Dover Beach." *Sandpoint News Bulletin*, August 2, 1978.

Kootenai County Republican. Editorial. October 25, 1901, 4.

Kusmin, Lorin. "Rural America at a Glance." Washington, DC: United States Department of Agriculture Economic Research Service, 2015. www.ers.usda.gov /webdocs/publications/44015/55581_eib145.pdf?v=0.

Lobsinger, Caroline. "City Debates Extending Services to Rocky Point." *Bonner County Daily Bee*, July 23, 1992.

———. "Dover Leaning toward Sewer District Takeover: City Negotiating with Rocky Point." *Coeur d'Alene Press*, January 14, 1996.

———. "Dover May Finalize Sewer Acquisition." *Bonner County Daily Bee*, June 4, 1996.

———. "Rocky Point Gains City Ear." *Bonner County Daily Bee*, July 29, 1992.

Loomis, Erik. *Empire of Timber: Labor Unions and the Pacific Northwest Forests*. New York: Cambridge University Press, 2016.

Lorah, Paul, and Rob Southwick. "Environmental Protection, Population Change, and Economic Development in the Rural Western United States." *Population and Environment* 24, no. 3 (2003): 255–72.

Lyons, Kevin. "Recognizing the Archaeological Signatures of Resident Fisheries: Considerations from the Pend Oreille Basin." In *Rivers, Fish, and the People: Tradition, Science, and Historical Ecology of Fisheries in the American West*, edited by Pei-Lin Yu, 96–126. Salt Lake City: University of Utah Press, 2015.

Mackenzie, Phillip [pseudonym]. "Development Hurts Dover, Community." *Bonner County Daily Bee*, August 3, 2004.

Malone, Michael P., and Richard W. Etulain. *The American West*. Lincoln, NE: Bison Books, 1989.

Marx, Karl. *Capital*. Vol. 1, translated by Ben Fowkes. New York: Penguin, 1990.

McCarthy, James. "Rural Geography: Globalizing the Countryside." *Progress in Human Geography* 32, no. 1 (2008): 129–37.

McLean, Mike. "Blaze Ravages Dover Mill." *Bonner County Daily Bee*, May 9, 1992.

———. "Cause of Fire at Dover Mill Identified." *Bonner County Daily Bee*, May 10, 1992.

———. "Firefighters Visit Mill Twice after Fire: Winds Stirs Up Burning Sawdust." *Bonner County Daily Bee*, May 12, 1992.

Nathan, Sarah. "The Bend: An Exploration of Community, Conservation and the Effects of Development in Middle Tennessee." Master's thesis, Syracuse University, 2015, www.thisisthebend.com.

Neiwert, David. "Dover Beach: Who Really Owns It? Is the Question." *Bonner County Daily Bee*, July 9, 1979.

Nelson, Lise, and Peter B. Nelson. "The Global Rural: Gentrification and Linked Migration in the Rural USA." *Progress in Human Geography* 35, no. 4 (2011): 441–59.

Nelson, Lise, Laurie Trautman, and Peter B. Nelson. "Latino Immigrants and Rural Gentrification: Race, 'Illegality,' and Precarious Labor Regimes in the United States." *Annals of the Association of American Geographers* 105, no. 4 (2015): 841–58.

Nelson, Peter, and J. Dwight Hines. "Rural Gentrification and Networks of Capital Accumulation—A Case Study of Jackson Hole, Wyoming." *Environment and Planning A: Economy and Space* 50, no. 7 (2018): 1473–95.

Nelson, Ted. "Dover Seeks End to Water System Woes." *Bonner County Daily Bee*, April 15, 1987.

New York Times. "Bombs Rock Idaho City Torn by Strife." September 30, 1986.

Nichols, Clare. "Dover Beach: Commissioners Suggest Means to End Conflict." *Bonner County Daily Bee*, August 3, 1978.

Nisbet, Jack. "'A Place to Build a House On': David Thompson, Kullyspel House and the Indian Meadows Tribal Encampment on Lake Pend Oreille." *Sandpoint Magazine* 19, no 2 (Summer 2009): 58–65.

Nokes, R. G. *Massacred for Gold: The Chinese in Hells Canyon.* Corvallis: Oregon State University Press, 2009.

North Idaho News Network. "Dover Water on—for Now." January 3, 1991.

Northern Idaho News. "Lumber Company Take Option on N.P. Land, Timber." May 19, 1944.

Northern Pacific Railroad Company. *Vast Areas of the Best Wheat Lands! Grazing Lands! Timber Lands! Gold and Silver Districts along the Line of the Northern Pacific Railroad* [. . .] *through Minnesota, Dakota, Montana, Idaho, Washington, and Oregon.* Chicago: Rand McNally, ca. 1883. https://babel.hathitrust.org/cgi/pt?id=njp.32101078192083&view=1up&seq=1.

Pend d'Oreille Review. "I.W.W Defense Starts; Defendants on Stand." January 30, 1920.

———. "The New Planer at the Dover Mill Starts Up." August 14, 1907.

———. "Portland Company Takes over White Lumber Co." November 7, 1929, 1.

Petersen, Erica [pseudonym]. "It's Not Over in Dover." *Bonner County Daily Bee,* December 30, 2004.

———. "[Mill Lake] Plan Not in City's Best Interests." *Bonner County Daily Bee,* August 8, 2004.

Peterson, Harold F. "Some Colonization Projects of the Northern Pacific Railroad." *Minnesota History* 10 no. 2 (1929): 127–44.

Phillips, Martin. "Counterurbanisation and Rural Gentrification: An Exploration of the Terms." *Population, Space and Place* 16, no. 6 (2010): 539–58.

Pilgeram, Ryanne. "'How Much Does Property Cost Up There?' Exploring the Relationship between Women, Sustainable Farming, and Rural Gentrification in the US." *Society and Natural Resources* 32, no. 8 (2019): 911–27.

Power, Thomas Michael. "Public Timber Supply, Market Adjustments, and Local Economies: Economic Assumptions of the Northwest Forest Plan." *Conservation Biology* 20, no. 2 (2006): 341–50.

Pullum, Jeri. "Beach Closure Angers Residents." *Bonner County Daily Bee,* July 24, 1978.

Renk, Nancy Foster. *A Glorious Field for Sawmills.* Boise: Idaho Transportation Department, 2014.

Richardson, Valerie. "Out on a Limb." *Washington Times,* November 25, 2001. www.washingtontimes.com/news/2001/nov/25/20011125-031421-1465r/.

Robbins, Paul, Katharine Meehan, Hannah Gosnell, and Susan J. Gilbertz. "Writing the New West: A Critical Review." *Rural Sociology* 74, no. 3 (2009): 356–82.

Sandpoint News Bulletin. "Interior Designers Enthusiastic about Board." August 7, 1955.

———. "New Water Tank at Dover Is Contemplated." May 11, 1951.

Sears, Roebuck and Co. *1897 Sears Roebuck Catalogue,* 1897. Accessed 2018. https://babel.hathitrust.org/cgi/pt?id=uc1.31158001963940&view=1up&seq=75.

Simmons, Eric A., Steven W. Hayes, Todd A. Morgan, Charles E. Keegan III, and Chris Witt. "Idaho's Forest Products Industry and Timber Harvest 2011 with Trends through 2013." *Resource Bulletin RMRS-RB-19* (2014): 1–46.

Smith, Neil. "Toward a Theory of Gentrification: A Back to the City Movement by Capital, Not People." *Journal of the American Planning Association* 45, no. 4 (1979): 538–48.

Stevens, Philip. "We Hold These Truths to Be Self-Evident." In *The New Deal Art Projects: Contemporary Encounters*, edited by Margaret E. Bullock, 159–63. Tacoma, WA: Tacoma Art Museum. 2020.

Stewart, Corenne. "Dover Beach Feud Ongoing." *Bonner County Daily Bee*, July 26, 2002.

Sutherland, Lee-Ann. "Return of the Gentleman Farmer? Conceptualising Gentrification in UK Agriculture." *Journal of Rural Studies* 28, no. 4 (2012): 568–76.

Turner, Dave. "Dover Residents Wary of Land Development: 800 New Homes Too Many for Area, Say Citizens." *Bonner County Daily Bee*, September 26, 1996.

———. "Judge Rules for City in Dover Development Flap." *Bonner County Daily Bee*, September 11, 1998.

Vukomanovic, Jelena. "Exurbia as Physical and Social Space: Landscape Drivers and Ecological Impacts of Amenity Migration in the New West." PhD diss., University of Arizona, 2013.

Ward, Sally. "Chronic Poverty, Community Decline, and Amenity-Rich Growth in Rural America: The Impact of Community Differences on Housing in Three Types of Rural Places." In *Rural Housing, Exurbanization, and Amenity-Driven Development Contrasting the "Haves" and the "Have Nots,"* edited by David Marcouiller, Mark Lapping, and Owen Furuseth, 157–74. Burlington, VT: Ashgate, 2010.

Wear, David N., and Brian C. Murray. "Federal Timber Restrictions, Interregional Spillovers, and the Impact on US Softwood Markets." *Journal of Environmental Economics and Management* 47 (2004): 307–30.

Weaver, Robert M., James C. Bard, and Mark S. Warner. *The Other Side of Sandpoint: Early History and Archaeology beside the Track: The Sandpoint Archaeology Project 2006–2013*. Vol. 3, *The Ethnography and Prehistory of Sandpoint*, edited by James C. Bard. Boise: Idaho Transportation Department, District 1, 2014.

Weber, Joe. "The Three American Wests." *Professional Geographer* 71, no. 2 (2019): 239–52.

Weyerhaeuser News Room. "Weyerhaeuser Declares Special Dividend, Marks Milestone in Planned Reit Conversion." July 11, 2010.

Winkler, Richelle, Donald R. Field, A. E. Luloff, Richard S. Krannich, and Tracy Williams. "Social Landscapes of the Inter-Mountain West: A Comparison of 'Old West' and 'New West' Communities." *Rural Sociology* 72, no. 3 (2007): 478–501.

Woods, Jeff. "Triumph of the Crunchy Granola People." *Nashville Scene*, September 4, 2008. www.nashvillescene.com/news/pith-in-the-wind/article/13016605/the-triumph-of-the-crunchy-granola-people.

Yaw, Raymond. "New More Facts." *Bonner County Daily Bee*, August 2, 1978.

INDEX

Page numbers in *italic* refer to illustrations.

parks and preserves, 118, 122, 125, 132
particleboard production, 44, 107
part-time residents. *See* second homes and second-home owners
paved trails, 128, *146*, 160
Pend Oreille people. *See* Kalispel (Pend Oreille) people
picnics, community. *See* community picnics
planned unit developments (PUDs), 80, 82, 88
population booms and busts, 13, 123–24, 125, 126, 150. *See also* "bypassed West"
prescriptive easement, 116
"private property" (concept), 141
property taxes, 73, 149
"protected West," 24, 121, 122, 125, 127
public beach access. *See* beaches and beach access
public health, 57, 107, 110
public hearings, 77, 80, 87, 89, 90, 94, 98, 99
public records. *See* archival records
public spaces. *See* commons (public spaces)
public trails, 128, *146*, 160

R

racial demographics and race relations, 34, 68–69
railroads, 32, 33–34, 35, 36, 39, 121, 122, 166
real estate investment trusts (REITs), 169
"rent gap," 50, 54, 168
resistance to development, 85–101, 106, 119, 170
restaurants, 34, 150, 154–55, 171
retirement, 124, 133, 150, 151, 153
rezoning. *See* zoning and rezoning
road construction, 54, 119, 136, 180–81n9 (ch. 6)
roadless areas. *See* wilderness

Roadless Wilderness Act, 53, 54
Robbins, Paul, 16
Rocky Point Sewer District, 73, 75, 93
Round Lake State Park, Idaho, 122
rubbish ordinances. *See* junk ordinances
Ruby Ridge standoff, 1992, 68
rural gentrification, 13–16, 18–25, 50, 149, 164

S

sabotage, 37, 38
Sagle, Idaho, 74, 121, 122
Salish people, 29, 30
Sandpoint, Idaho, ix–x, 14, 122, 153, 159, 171, 174; annexation question, 73–75; Aryan Nations, 68; bedroom communities, xi, 159; Dover rivalry, 74; early history, 33, 34, 35–36; Mark Fuhrman, 69; public meetings, 89; sewer system, 73–74
sawdust piles, 65, 107, 108, 135, 143; mill fires and, 62, 63
Saxton, Rufus, 31, 32
scarcity, 127, 140
seasonal jobs, 150–51
second homes and second-home owners, 84, 140, 152, 153
service-sector jobs, 150–51, 162
Seth, Shirley, 174
sewer systems, 66, 71, 72–76, 88, 93
Shamrock Investment Company, 70–72, 73, 75–83, 88, 93–94, 119, 167–68; beach access and, 112, 115; water system and, 56, 57, 58, 60–62, 63. *See also* Dover Development
Silver Valley, 38, 48, 124
skiing, 132, 133, 153, 163
snow plowing, 158
social class. *See* class
Southwick, Rob, 140
"spatial fix" (Harvey), 16–18, 86, 123, 164, 165, 168–69